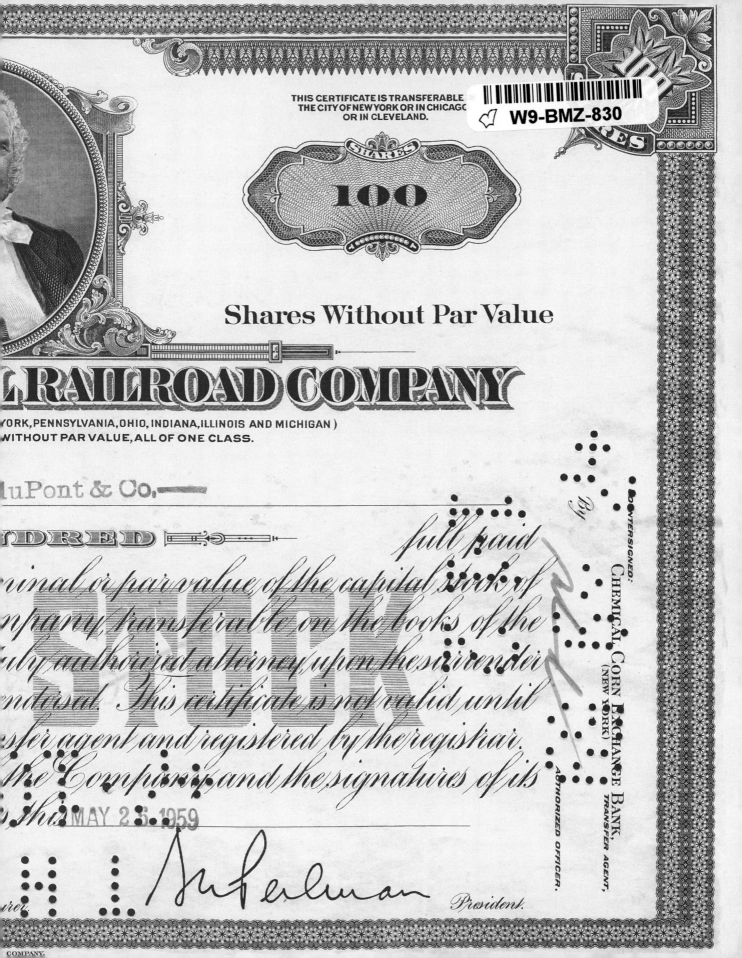

THIS CERTIFICATE IS TRANSFERABLE
THE CITY OF NEW YORK OR IN CHICAGO
OR IN CLEVELAND.

SHARES

100

Shares Without Par Value

L RAILROAD COMPANY

YORK, PENNSYLVANIA, OHIO, INDIANA, ILLINOIS AND MICHIGAN)
WITHOUT PAR VALUE, ALL OF ONE CLASS.

uPont & Co,

DRED

full paid

inal or par value of the capital stock of

npany, transferable on the books of the

ly authorized attorney upon the surrender

ndorsed. This certificate is not valid until

fer agent and registered by the registrar.

the Company and the signatures of its

MAY 2 5 1959

President.

COUNTERSIGNED:

CHEMICAL CORN EXCHANGE BANK,
(NEW YORK)
TRANSFER AGENT,

By

AUTHORIZED OFFICER.

COMPANY.

December 1999

Howard + Uveen

Thanks for your continued
Confidence. Best wishes for
The new Year !! .

John Burr

ALSO BY CHARLES R. GEISST

Wall Street: A History

CHARLES DOW

FURNISHED BY THE
TELEGRAPH
LOCAL MANAGER.

MARCH 17, 1903

100 YEARS OF WALL STREET

Charles R. Geisst

McGRAW-HILL

*New York   San Francisco   Washington, D.C.   Auckland   Bogotá
Caracas   Lisbon   London   Madrid   Mexico City   Milan
Montreal   New Dehli   San Juan   Singapore
Sydney   Tokyo   Toronto*

C. W. BARRON

Library of Congress Catalog Card Number 99-74662

McGraw-Hill

A Division of The McGraw·Hill Companies

1 2 3 4 5 6 7 8 9 0   CCW/CCW   9 0 9 8 7 6 5 4 3 2 1 0 9

ISBN 0-07-135619-3

DESIGNED BY BTDnyc

This book was set in Granjon, with Engravers LH and Copperplate Gothic.
Printed and bound by Courier Westford.

for Margaret

CONTENTS

FOREWORD

FOR MORE THAN 100 YEARS, THE "FATHER of our nation" has proudly and dutifully watched over Wall Street. From atop the steps of Federal Hall, where George Washington took the oath of office in 1789, the famous bronze likeness of America's first president has, in a manner of speaking, seen it all.

The eyes of this larger-than-life casting, watched the Exchange move into our current headquarters on Broad Street in 1903. They've witnessed the market crash of 1929 followed by the struggle, despair, and reform that was the Great Depression. Years later, they shared the joy and celebration with the arrival of the end of World War II and the post-war period of economic prosperity.

Then, seemingly overnight, they viewed another revolution of sorts: an equity revolution. Indeed, the American public—with renewed confidence in Wall Street and newfound enthusiasm for equity ownership—changed the very landscape of the capital marketplace. At the dawn of the second half of the twentieth century, the stage was now set for America to become a nation of shareholders.

In 1952, when an average day saw 1.3 million shares changing hands, just four percent of the U.S. population, or 6.5 million people, invested in the stock market. At that year's end, the NYSE's market capitalization totaled $120 million and the Dow Jones Industrial Average closed at a 291.90.

OPPOSITE

A Christmas tree stands in front of the New York Stock Exchange building on Wall Street in New York Monday, Dec. 18, 1995, the day that trading activity was postponed for an hour due to a computer system problem. It was the first such delay in nearly five years.

That same year, the Exchange embarked on a far-reaching educational campaign to increase public ownership. Launched under the aegis of NYSE president G. Keith Funston, the program was called *Own Your Share of American Business* and included a wide range of market education efforts and public information programs. The Exchange also launched a program allowing individuals to invest as little as $40 per month in the market through special accounts at NYSE member firms. The Exchange, too, campaigned for legislation permitting institutional buyers to increase their investments in listed securities.

The early results were impressive. By the end of the 1950s, direct ownership of stocks had nearly doubled to 12.5 million. From that base, the trend toward ownership of business by a broad base of the American public grew rapidly: 20 million by 1965, 30 million by 1970, 40 million by 1985, more than 51 million by 1990.

By 1999, nearly 80 million individual investors directly own publicly traded securities, with tens of millions more participating indirectly through pension and mutual funds. Moreover, the level of public participation has grown to more than 30 percent of the overall population and more than 40 percent among adults.

At the same time, the Exchange has grown to become the world's largest and liquid equities marketplace. Our 3,100 listed companies, the world's best, represent a total market capitalization of more than $16 trillion. Nearly 800 million shares trade each day, with the billion-dollar share day a reality. Dow 10,000 and 11,000 are now the milestones of market performance.

The American investor has spawned an equity culture so unique to our world, so vital to our economic well being. Its scope and depth serve as the foundation for the capital marketplace, and the model for both developed and newly emerging markets. It's the source of capital necessary for businesses to innovate and expand, to turn ideas into realities, while enabling investors to build their savings and improve their standard of living.

The story of Wall Street in the twentieth century is the story of the American investing public and of the confidence in equity investing that has made ours the world's largest nation of shareholders. It's a story that, at its start, no one could have foretold. Now, at the close of this century, it's a legendary saga—of unprecedented growth and participation…of America serving as the cornerstone of the global ecomony…of Wall Street and Main Street becoming one.

As we enter the new millennium, my partners and I at the Exchange and throughout Wall Street community remain steadfast in our commitment to the investing public. We are in the business of supporting all shareowners and safeguarding their interests…by providing a market of the highest quality, by applying the most advanced technology and practices, and ensuring the highest standards of integrity and regulatory oversight.

As we turn the page to write another chapter in the history of Wall Street, it's only fitting to celebrate America's equity culture…with the knowledge that the American dream born of the vision of our nation's forefathers is more promising than ever.

RICHARD A. GRASSO
Chairman and Chief Executive Officer
New York Stock Exchange

The World
Financial Center
from New Jersey.

The New York Stock
Exchange.

INTRODUCTION

AT THE TURN OF THE TWENTIETH century, Wall Street and the country were brimming over with optimism. Ever since the New York Stock Exchange had its unofficial start with the Buttonwood Agreement in 1791, the financial world had been growing and Wall Street was acknowledged as the home of the country's financial markets. Interest in investment was growing, and so were many new companies. The new technologies—the telephone and heavy manufacturing to name just two—intrigued investors and attracted even more money to the markets. By the outbreak of World War I, the United States was no longer an emerging power. It now ranked along with the European countries as a first-rate military and economic power.

Still Wall Street was not a bed of roses for investors. Severe market downturns, known as "panics" during the nineteenth century, continued to plague the market and caused recessions and depressions. In the late 1800s, strong individuals dominated the large banks and brokerage firms and made an indelible imprint upon the market. Figures such as J. P. Morgan, Jay Gould, August Belmont, and Cornelius Vanderbilt all made their fortunes in finance and were larger-than-life individuals on the Street. They had the power and influence to sway markets, and on more than one occasion they were blamed for causing panics for their

OPPOSITE

The Buttonwood Agreement in 1792 was the first attempt by traders in what was an outdoor market to organize themselves. The agreement was signed under a Buttonwood tree on Wall Street after the first major scandal involving speculation caused many outdoor traders and banks to fail. The rules that it included became the basis for the founding of the New York Stock and Exchange Board some years later.

J.P. Morgan, Wall Street's most powerful figure, in 1904.

own greedy ends. As the twentieth century began, their influence was still felt directly and indirectly. Wall Street was still known for its strong personalities and lack of financial regulation. However, the environment would change significantly over the course of the century.

The changes that Wall Street witnessed during the twentieth century were inconceivable in 1900. Although the New York Stock Exchange had made significant strides in its own development, the other New York stock market, the Curb Exchange, was still conducted out-of-doors along Broad Street. On a good day, the NYSE traded several hundred thousand shares. On a bad day, it could trade significantly less. No one imagined days when over a billion shares would change hands, as they did in the late 1990s. In 1900, AT&T was not yet formed. By the end of the century, trading had moved to the Internet, bypassing the telephone as a preferred method of trading.

Some of the most momentous changes affecting the Street concerned how it did business. In 1900, the markets were unregulated, with only sparse exchange rules and regulations governing trades. The Crash of 1929 was more severe than panics before it and caused widespread damage across the country. Wall Street tried in vain to buttress itself, as bankers attempted to stabilize the market, but without success. Within four years, FDR's administration enacted the first nationwide securities and banking laws intended to ensure that another crash did not occur. In the words of Will Rogers, the Street found itself with a cop on the corner for the first time in its 150-year history.

The Depression had taken its toll on Wall Street in more than one respect. After losing money during and after the Crash, many investors became disenchanted by Senate hearings concerning the Crash that revealed much about the inner workings of the Street. The combination of losing money and finding out how Wall Street really worked caused such widespread displeasure that investors stayed away from investments for almost two decades. Brokers achieved the dubious distinction of becoming one of the least regarded professions in the country.

Small investors only returned to Wall Street in the 1950s. The post-war boom created a new generation of investors who had forgotten the days of the Depression. Investors again became attracted to stocks, especially those that were related to the cold war. Defense-related stocks led the market higher, and the market managed to exceed the levels established before the Crash. By 1972, the Dow Jones Industrial Average reached a milestone when it broke 1,000 for the first time. But the market ran out of steam, and a long bear market followed, prompted by rising oil prices and inflation. The market retreated below 1,000 and remained depressed during the late 1970s and early 1980s.

After a volatile history, the market began what would become the biggest bull market in its 200-year history in the early 1980s. It was accompanied by the largest merger boom of the century as well. The cold war ended with the fall of Soviet Communism, and the markets began to rise to unprecedented levels. Mutual funds became the most popular form of investment for many investors, and eventually there were more funds in existence than individual stocks. At the end of the century, the Dow had crossed the 10,000 barrier. When compared with the meager 100 that the index registered in the early 1900s, Wall Street could happily claim that the entire century had been one of a great bull market.

The Laclede Gas & Light Company, an early power company, was one of the original components of the Dow 12 Average. Preferred stock was often more popular than commonstock with investors because of its dividends.

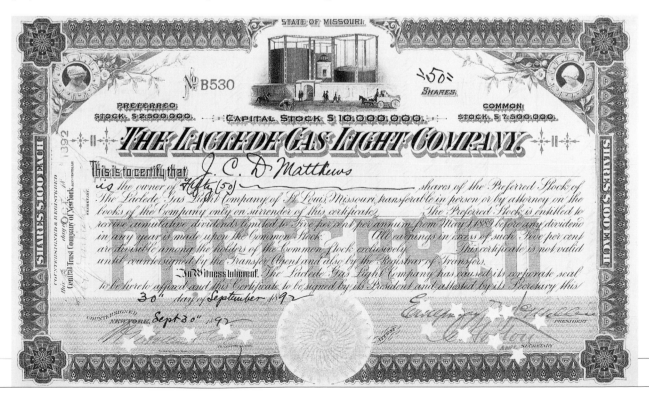

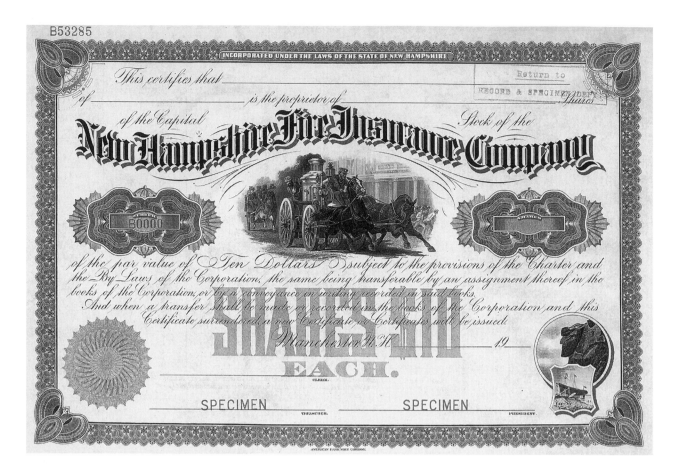

Insurance was one of the nineteenth- century favorites for investors. Life insurance became extremely popular after the Civil War.

But the story of Wall Street in the twentieth century is not only one of finance. Being the most recognizable street name in the country, and perhaps the world, brought with it celebration and tragedy. While the rest of the country endured Prohibition, the number of speakeasies in lower Manhattan proliferated. Having a good time has always been a Wall Street tradition, and there were numerous occasions in the century to celebrate. Wall Street has always liked to throw parties, and the ticker tape parades it has held over the years have honored some of the best known public figures and heroes from around the world.

Over the years, Wall Street also became a target for terrorists. Since the First World War, bombs have exploded in and around the financial district, bringing terror and sometimes death. The capital of capitalism always attracted attention from those intent on making a point. Sometimes the attacks were personally motivated, but in most cases they were political, aimed at the financial district in general rather than at anyone in particular.

As the stock market indices rose over the years, the Street also became a tourist magnet. Until the early 1920s, the crowds on Broad and Wall were mainly those of the brokers who made up the curb market, the forerunner of the American Stock Exchange. When they finally moved indoors in 1921, the thoroughfare turned into something of a tourist mecca. The happy days of the 1920s drew crowds to the Street, as small investors clamored to see capitalism at work. When the market crashed in 1929, people poured into the area to see firsthand what had happened to the giddy marketplace. The pattern has been followed many times. The market's collapse in 1987 drew crowds to the New York Stock Exchange's gallery. This time, however, the morbid curiosity seekers would be disappointed, because a crash had been replaced by only a temporary, but severe, sell-off. The market soon would resume its upward trend to break new historic levels. Unlike the nineteenth century, the twentieth experienced fewer crashes, panics, and bear markets.

The twentieth century began full of promise as the United States and Wall Street slowly started to find their way in the world. The twenty-first century begins on another note of optimism. Instead of looking for investments in railroads and early telephone companies, the emphasis has changed to investments in communications and other high-tech industries that would have baffled even a science fiction writer 100 years ago.

Lionel Corporation, the maker of model railroad trains, was a favorite of investors and children in the 1950s.

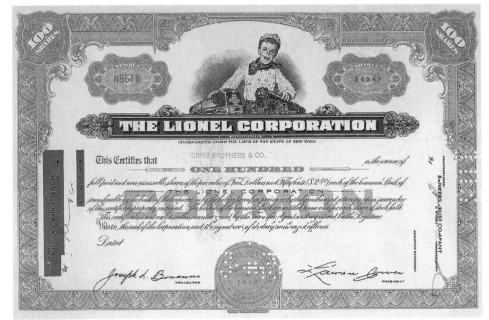

A prankster chained a teddy bear to the statue of Wall Street's famous bull in the summer of 1998, during a bad month in the market.

The photos that follow, telling Wall Street's history over the course of the twentieth century, illustrate how the Street progressed from a relatively insular place where bucket shops operated in the shadow of large private banks to the giant marketplace that has

brought trillions of dollars' worth of capital to market. Serious moments have always existed alongside the lighthearted on the world's most famous street, and only pictures can capture the spirit of both.

CHARLES R. GEISST

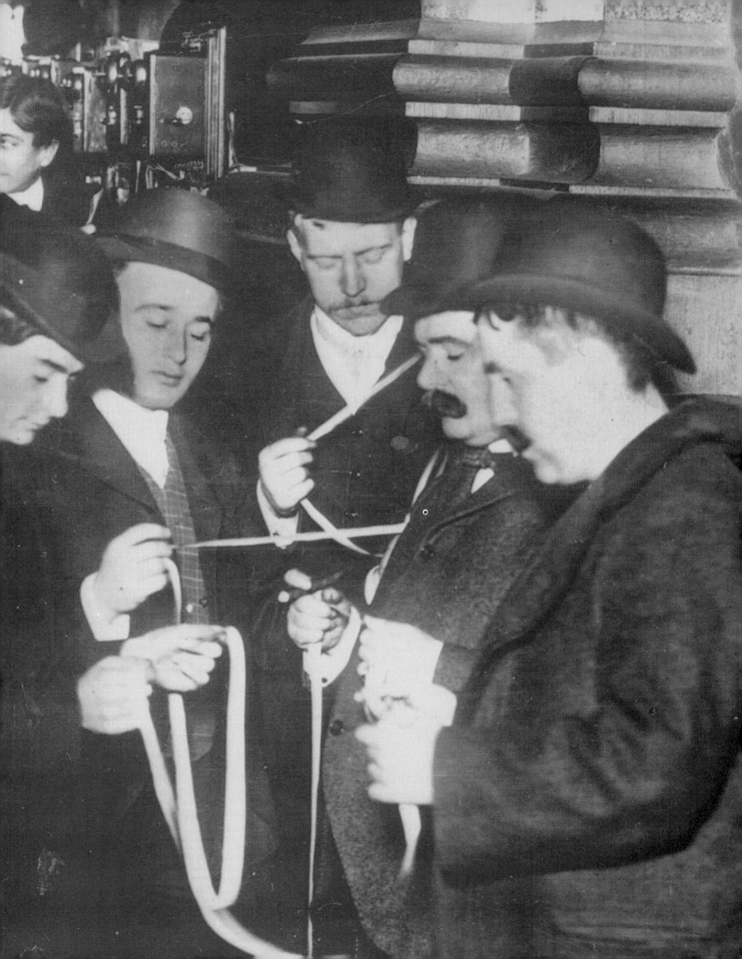

ACKNOWLEDGMENTS

SPECIAL THANKS TO THE STAFFS OF The Associated Press/Wide World Photos, the Museum of American Financial History, and the Underwood Photo Archives, and especially Lisa Underwood, for helping me assemble the photos contained in the book. Nancy Mikhail, executive editor at McGraw-Hill, was instrumental in holding the project together and keeping it on track. Without all of their efforts, the book would have never succeeded.

OPPOSITE

The ticker tape, invented by Thomas Edison, was the first method brokers had of checking stock prices on a regular basis. Here, several brokers at the turn of the century study prices closely.

THE 1900s AND "TEENS"

AS THE TWENTIETH CENTURY BEGAN, America was in a buoyant mood. The country was emerging as a world leader in manufacturing, farming, and technological developments. Republican William McKinley was in the White House, and his policies were sympathetic to big business. Although no one could foresee the momentous changes that the economy, and Wall Street, would witness over the next 100 years, the century began very much as it would eventually end, in the midst of a tremendous merger boom.

After McKinley was assassinated in 1901, Teddy Roosevelt became president and the twentieth century was officially in high gear. Wall Street was witnessing mergers between companies that no one thought possible and at prices that were incomprehensible. J. P. Morgan bought Carnegie Steel from its founder, Andrew Carnegie, for $500 million, a record amount that left even Wall Street financiers breathless. The amount was so huge that Carnegie decided to give much of it to charity and other worthwhile causes. Morgan's reputation as the major financier on Wall Street was also strengthened, and he went on to forge other large companies, among them American Telephone & Telegraph, the Northern Securities Company, and International Harvester. Before

OPPOSITE

*W*all Street at the turn of the twentieth century was a busy thoroughfare. This scene looks west toward Trinity Church (in the background). Most of the people on the street are messengers and runners, traveling by foot and by wagon. Since the days when Peter Stuyvesant first built the wall to protect the street from the local Indians and English adventurers, Wall Street has been one of the few east-west arteries in lower Manhattan.

World War I, his salary was estimated at a staggering $5 million per year, equivalent to an even more staggering $3 billion today.

These enormous mergers set the tone for the century to follow. Industry was consolidating, and trusts, or monopolies, appeared everywhere. Many tried to emulate Rockefeller's Standard Oil Trust as the business organization of the future. Fear of these huge companies began a trust-busting trend that lasted until the beginning of the 1920s. Society and business were changing rapidly, and no one was sure that these enormous companies could be trusted to act responsibly toward their workers and consumers.

Wall Street was not the friendliest place for the small investor before the First World War. Artists traditionally depicted the Street as a place where bulls *fought* bears. And the results could be bloody. Competition was often fierce. The bulls would have their day by running prices up, and eventually the bears would have theirs, by forcing prices down. Bull raids and bear raids on the exchange floor typified the investment environment. Investors who were caught in the middle often suffered badly. The atmosphere changed once war was declared, but it resumed during the 1920s in a slightly more sophisticated manner.

The Bulls & Bears game was one of the first board games, reflecting an interest in investing well before the turn of the century. Developed in 1883, the game was one of the most popular for years after.

Two major stock market panics occurred before 1910. The first took place in 1903 as a result of the wild speculation that followed the creation of U.S. Steel. But its repercussions were not long lasting. The second panic occurred in 1907, causing widespread ruin on Wall Street. Several banks and brokers were forced to the wall. The investment bankers teamed up with the U.S. Treasury to bail out several institutions that oth-

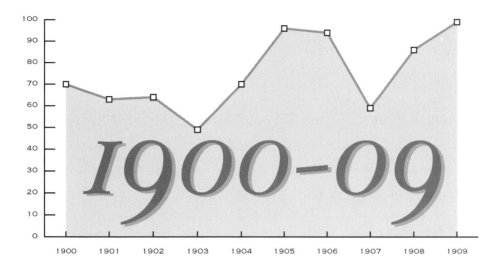

erwise might have failed. J. P. Morgan led the effort. And because of his efforts, the NYSE was able to remain open. Brokers applauded him as their savior, but he was criticized more than praised by those outside Wall Street.

The country had had its share of panics and financial failures and desperately needed some stability. Progressive politicians maintained that the Street manufactured the panics to make money on the cleanup operations that followed. While no one could prove it, one fact was certain: Wall Street was still acting as if it were in the nineteenth century. And it lost its elder statesman when J. Pierpont Morgan died in 1913. He was succeeded at the bank bearing his name by his son, Jack.

Teddy Roosevelt's administration filed suit against several huge companies that had been created in the previous twenty years. John D. Rockefeller's Standard Oil and James B. Duke's American Tobacco were both sued for being monopolies, and their cases went before the Supreme Court. And Congress investigated Wall Street and its bankers in 1912. The Pujo hearings of 1912 brought some of Wall Street's top bankers into the public eye for the first time. One by one, Wall Street's elite told Congress that they had no idea what all the fuss was about concerning panics and monopolies despite the fact that in 1911 the Supreme Court ordered the breakup of both Standard Oil and American Tobacco.

The extent of Wall Street's influence was made public by the hearings. Shortly after, Congress created the Federal Reserve, and Wall Street had to come to terms with the new central bank. But unlike the Fed under its better known chairmen in the latter part of the century, the new institution was still overshadowed by the major bankers and brokers. Then war broke out in Europe, casting a dark shadow over the markets. The stock markets were closed for the last quarter of 1914 even though the United States did not enter the war until 1917. When they reopened, the averages rose. America did not want to go to war, and investors celebrated. The party lasted about two years.

Investing in stocks was a risky business prior to the 1920s. Brokers were mainly small and varied by reputation. Small investors often were taken in by bucket shops. These fly-by-night investment dealers would allow a small investor to buy some stock for only a small percentage of its price—buying "on margin." It would take the order but usually put its own order in to the exchange first so that the investors' orders drove

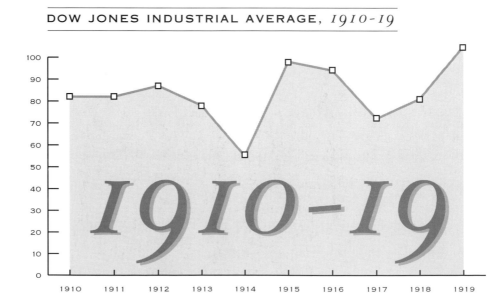

DOW JONES INDUSTRIAL AVERAGE, *1910-19*

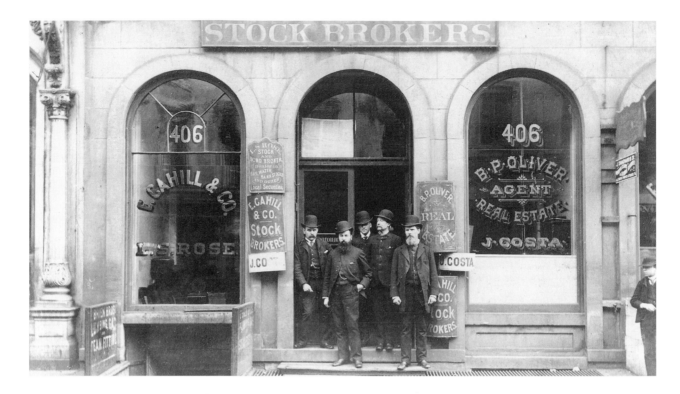

up the price. Many small investors made a short-term killing with the bucket shops, but many more lost substantial amounts dealing with them. One of Wall Street's major tasks was to rid itself of these shady operators so that its public image would improve.

Trying to stop brokers and insiders from preying on the investing public began to gain some momentum during the war years. After the Pujo hearings, Congress started an investigation into stock market practices. And the *New York Times* began offering rewards for anyone placing misleading financial ads in the newspaper that could influence the price of a stock. Since the days of Jay Gould in the 1870s and 1880s, planted stories given to journalists had been a favorite way for manipulators to move the price of a stock up or down.

The "teens" became one of the most momentous decades of the twentieth century. In addition to the breakup of the two giant monopolies (Standard Oil and American Tobacco), the congressional hearings, and the creation of the Federal Reserve, the *Titanic* sank in 1912, taking with it many notable financiers. The income tax was introduced in 1913.

Although the stock exchange was well established, many small brokers existed who were not affiliated with it, and selling stocks and bonds was not much different from selling real estate or other assets. Even the small brokers advertised the sort of stocks they specialized in. Many of these small businesses, called bucket shops, often used investors' money to run up the price of a stock, benefiting themselves before their investors.

Wall Street and many major industrialists were not amused by the prospect of having to pay tax on their earnings. And the market took a downward turn when the United States finally entered the war, having one of its worst years ever in 1917. Adding to Wall Street's woes was the influenza epidemic of 1918 that killed almost 20 million people worldwide. The Street was desperately in need of good news when the war ended in 1918. It was time for a celebration.

Just as the war ended, the Prohibition Amendment was passed. One of the Street's favorite pastimes was now officially outlawed, although, as the 1920s would prove, that did not dampen the enthusiasm for a drink. Opening speakeasies became a major "growth" industry in and around the Street. As everyone was fond of saying, having a drink was not illegal, only manufacturing it was. Al Capone would take the place of financiers as one of the most highly compensated heads of a "syndicate" in the country. And the financial world had reason to celebrate as the 1920s approached. The Supreme Court refused to break up U.S. Steel in a famous lawsuit brought by the government, and the market had broken the Dow 100 level for only the third time since 1906.

The 1920s were just around the corner. After years of war and change, the decade of excess was poised to roar in, throwing caution to the wind.

How much is it worth today?

Over the course of the century, the stock and bond markets have fluctuated widely in price. Many times, comparisons can be made in current dollars against what the same investment would have been worth 100 years ago. Dow Jones estimates that if an investor had invested $10,000 in the stock market in 1900 and kept it invested, it would be worth $90 million today. That sounds easier than it might have been since many of the original companies listed on the exchange no longer exist or were merged with others.

At the turn of the century, the New York Stock Exchange was the largest in the country. Here, the members of the Boston Stock Exchange pose for a photo at the "Atchison" pole, the place where railroad shares were traded.

APRIL FOOL

In 1916, German agents were suspected of setting off the munitions dump, known as Black Tom, located across the Hudson River in Jersey City, New Jersey. The facility was almost entirely destroyed and the explosion was so powerful that it blew out most windows on Wall Street. It was the second recorded instance of German terrorism affecting the Street. A few years before, a German agent attempted to shoot Jack Morgan at his home in Long Island but was subdued and arrested. Morgan himself escaped with only minor wounds.

OPPOSITE

Small investors were considered fair game for stock market traders in the early part of the century. Here, a trader, or "operator," plays the old "come on" game with an unsuspecting small speculator, trying to lure him and his money.

STOCKS TO LEAD THE WORLD

At the turn of the century, the Dow Jones Industrial Average was only four years old. Charles Dow included the following twelve companies in his index: American Cotton Oil, American Sugar, American Tobacco, Chicago Gas, Distilling & Cattle Feeding, General Electric, Laclede Gas, National Lead, North American, Tennessee Iron & Coal, U.S. Leather Preferred, and U.S. Rubber.

LEFEVRE, THE WHISTLE

In the 1920s, well-known broker Edwin Lefevre wrote in his widely read book, *Reminiscences of a Stock Operator,* that the infamous bucket shops that enticed so many unwitting investors were on the wane. "The old fashioned bucket shops are gone though bucketeering brokerage houses still prosper at the expense of men and women who persist in playing the game of getting rich quick" he wrote. Many investors would have agreed with him, especially after the Crash of 1929 when the borrowed money, called margin money, used to buy stocks on credit, was responsible for the ruin of many investors.

OPPOSITE

The curb market flourished outdoors until 1921 when it finally moved indoors to its home on Trinity Place, several blocks from the New York Stock Exchange. It finally changed its name to the American Stock Exchange in 1951. Here, brokers are seen congregating outside the NYSE in 1917. They often would look to the NYSE for investment information, which traveled quickly by word of mouth among the brokers.

OVERLEAF

Wall Street became accustomed to giving parades in the nineteenth century. The last parade of the century was given for Admiral Dewey after his victory at Manila Bay in the Spanish American War. In 1919, another was given for General Pershing and the American Expeditionary Force after their return from Europe following World War I. Also honored was Sergeant Alvin York, the Tennessee sharpshooter whose heroics claimed many enemy lives. He was later immortalized in a movie bearing his name.

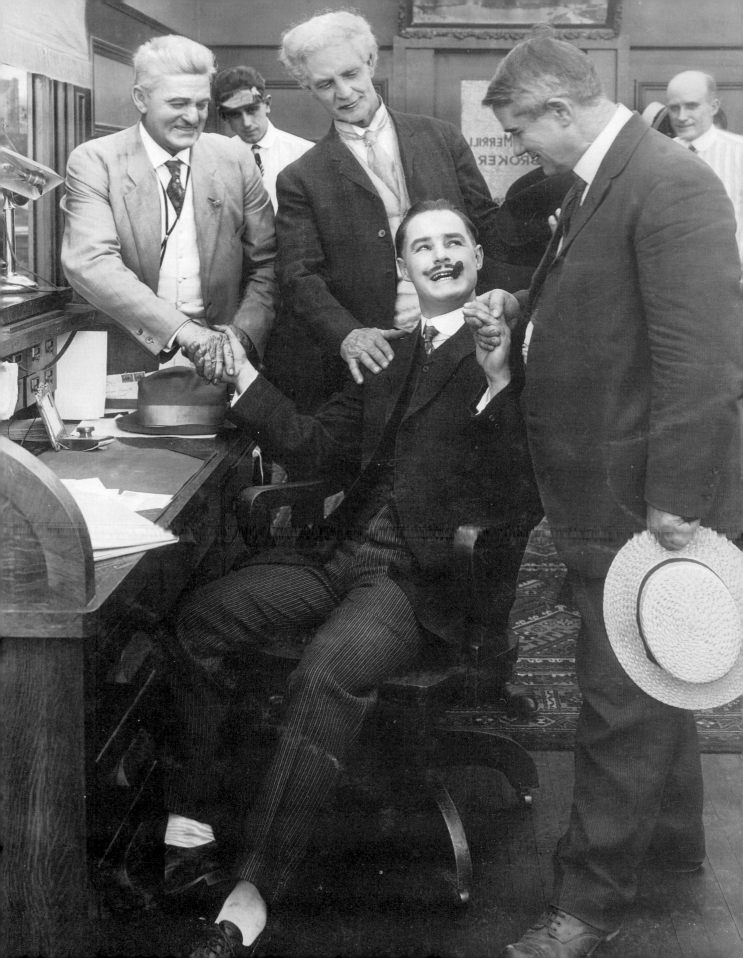

THE ROARING TWENTIES

THE 1920S IRONICALLY WITNESSED Wall Street's finest and worst hours. The decade began on a sour note, experienced a boom, and then disintegrated into chaos all within the course of just nine years. This legacy lives on at the end of the century and will reach far into the twenty-first as well.

After the war, the economy slumped into a recession until 1921. Then things began to turn around. The Jazz Age of flappers and illegal booze began. Many consumers started to benefit from new products and postwar prosperity. They began to buy new cars, homes, and radios—the new mass technological development—and the economy prospered. At the end of the war, owning a radio was rare. By 1929, over 10 million homes had at least one. Consumers bought more and more new cars and also began using the telephone in record numbers. One of their usual phone calls was to their broker.

Wall Street quickly noticed the trend. Brokers began marketing themselves to the public as never before. They placed ads in magazines and newspapers advertising their investment skills. And the large banks were also involved. Many bought brokers in order to participate in the boom. Brokers were mostly local. The large "wire houses" were still in

USE A LITTLE
WINE FOR THY
STOMACH'S SAKE

I TIMOTHY 5ᵗʰ CHAPTER 23ᵈ VERSE

Anti-Prohibitionists found Wall Street a receptive place for a parade. While the rest of the country was dry, Wall Street had enough speakeasies to accommodate everyone who wanted a drink. Here, an antitemperance wagon preaches the use of a little wine for purely "medicinal" purposes.

their infancy, and the idea of reaching the public through branch offices was still new. Banks like the National City Bank of New York opened hundreds of securities branches connected by almost 12,000 miles of communications wires. Its chief executive, Charles Mitchell, became one of the most vocal proponents of investing for everyone. The "financial department store" became the buzzword of the decade among brokers. If customers could not come to you, open a branch and go to them. The stock market boom was beginning.

The 1920s was a decade of speculation in general. A Florida land boom began before the stock market rally, with crooked real estate agents selling useless, mosquito-ridden land in interior Florida. Charles Ponzi, the father of the "Ponzi scheme," made a fortune selling bogus real estate there to an unsuspecting public. Stockbrokers were extremely happy because the investing public discovered stocks for the first time on a large scale. More and more people wanted to speculate in

ABOVE

I n the 1920s, many banks and brokers ran ads showing their financial prowess and advisory capabilities. The best known campaign was mounted by the National City Bank, the predecessor of Citibank today. Its affiliate, the National City Company, marketed its services to the growing managerial and middle classes. Most of its business was originally aimed at bond investors, and it only became involved with stocks toward the latter part of the decade.

O ne of Wall Street's best known personalities of the 1920s was Charles Mitchell of National City Bank in New York. The architect of the bank's aggressive plunge into the brokerage business, Mitchell was one of the most outspoken bulls of the decade. He is seen here on a Cunard Line ship, examining the brokerage facilities set up by Michael Meehan, the floor trader best known for successfully organizing many investment pools operating on the floor of the NYSE.

OPPOSITE

After the curb market moved indoors to its new home on Trinity Place, the crowds of traders disappeared from the front of the NYSE. Here, two young boys, from their vantage point of the old Subtreasury Building, look down at the corner of Broad Street and Wall.

the market in order to get rich quick, and there were many brokers willing to accommodate them.

The 1920s were also years of salesmanship. Everyone was selling something, and Wall Street was no exception. Madison Avenue advertising was coming into its own, and the Street began to borrow some of its methods in order to project a serious image to potential investors. The image that Wall Street attempted to create for itself would soon backfire, however, when the Crash occurred in 1929.

Wall Street became a more sophisticated place in the 1920s. The markets handled greater turnover in stocks and bonds, the number of people employed by brokers increased, and new investment products were developed. The New York Curb Exchange moved indoors in 1921 so that it could provide some competition for the NYSE. The over-the-counter market, the predecessor of the NASDAQ, also began to organize, selling the stocks of companies not listed on the exchanges. The markets began to welcome smaller investors. The exchanges began to move away from being places where professional traders dominated the action. The Dow Jones Industrial Average expanded to thirty stocks in

Everybody Ought to be Rich

An Interview With John J. Raskob

By SAMUEL CROWTHER

BEING rich is, of course, a comparative status. A man with a million dollars used to be considered rich, but so many people have at least that much in these days, or are earning incomes in excess of a normal return from a million dollars, that a millionaire does not cause any comment.

Fixing a bulk line to define riches is a pointless performance. Let us rather say that a man is rich when he has an income from invested capital which is sufficient to support him and his family in a decent and comfortable manner—to give as much support, let us say, as has ever been given by his earnings. That amount of prosperity ought to be attainable by anyone. A greater share will come to those who have greater ability.

It seems to me to be a primary duty for people to make it their business to understand how wealth is produced and not to take their ideas from writers and speakers who have the gift of words but not the gift of ordinary common sense. Wealth is not created in dens of iniquity, and it is much more to the point to understand what it is all about than to listen to the expounding of new systems which at the best can only make worse the faults of our present system.

It is quite true that wealth is not so evenly distributed as it ought to be and as it can be. And part of the reason for the unequal distribution is the lack of systematic investment and also the lack of even moderately sensible investment.

One class of investors saves money and puts it into savings banks or other mediums that pay only a fixed interest. Such funds are valuable, but they do not lead to wealth. A second class tries to get rich all at once, and buys any wildcat security that comes along with the promise of immense returns. A third class holds that the return from interest is not enough to justify savings, but at the same time has too much sense to buy fake stocks—and so saves nothing at all. Yet all the while wealth has been here for the asking.

The common stocks of this country have in the past ten years increased enormously in value because the business of the country has increased. Ten thousand dollars invested ten years ago in the common stock of General Motors would now be worth more than a million and a half dollars. And General Motors is only one of many first-class industrial corporations.

It may be said that this is a phenomenal increase and that conditions are going to be different in the next ten years. That prophecy may be true, but it is not founded on experience. In my opinion the wealth of the country is bound to increase at a very rapid rate. The rapidity of the rate will be determined by the increase in consumption, and under wise investment plans the consumption will steadily increase.

We Have Scarcely Started

NOW anyone may regret that he or she did not have ten thousand dollars ten years ago and did not put it into General Motors or some other good company—and sigh over a lost opportunity. Anyone who firmly believes that the opportunities are all closed and that from now on the country will get worse instead of better is welcome to the opinion—and to whatever increment it will bring. I think that we have scarcely started, and I have thought so for many years.

In conjunction with others I have been interested in creating and directing at least a dozen trusts for investment in equity securities. This plan of equity investments is no mere theory with me. The first of these trusts was started in 1907 and the others in the years immediately following. Under all of these the plan provided for the saving of fifteen dollars per month for investment in equity securities only. There were no stocks bought on margin, no money borrowed, nor any stocks bought for a quick turn or resale. All stocks with few exceptions have been bought and held as permanent investments. The fifteen dollars was saved every month and the dividends from the stocks purchased were kept in the trust and reinvested. Three of these trusts are now twenty years old. Fifteen dollars per month equals one hundred and eighty dollars a year. In twenty years, therefore, the total savings amounted to thirty-six hundred dollars. Each of these three trusts is now worth well in excess of eighty thousand dollars. Invested at 6 per cent interest, this eighty thousand dollars would give the trust beneficiary an annual income of four hundred dollars per month, which ordinarily would represent more than the earning power of the beneficiary, because had he been able to earn as much as four hundred dollars per month he could have saved more than fifteen dollars.

Suppose a man marries at the age of twenty-three and begins a regular saving of fifteen dollars a month—and almost anyone who is employed can do that if he tries. If he invests in good common stocks and allows the dividends and rights to accumulate, he will at the end of twenty years have at least eighty thousand dollars and an income from investments of around four hundred dollars a month. And because anyone can do that I am firm in my belief that anyone not only can be rich but ought to be rich.

The obstacles to being rich are two: The trouble of saving, and the trouble of finding a medium for investment.

If Tom is known to have two hundred dollars in the savings bank then everyone is out to get it for some absolutely necessary purpose. More than likely his wife's sister will eventually find the emergency to draw it forth. But if he does withstand all attacks, what good will the money do him? The interest he receives is so small that he has no incentive to save, and since the whole is under his jurisdiction he can depend only upon his own will to save. To save in any such fashion requires a stronger will than the normal.

If he thinks of investing in some stock he has nowhere to turn for advice. He is not big enough to get much attention from his banker, and he has not enough money to go to a broker—or at least he thinks that he has not.

Suppose he has a thousand dollars; the bank can only advise him to buy a bond, for the officer will not take the risk of advising a stock and probably has not the experience anyway to give such advice. Tom can get really adequate attention only from some man who has a worthless security to sell, for then all of Tom's money will be profit.

The plan that I have had in mind for several years grows out of the success of the plans that we have followed for the executives in the General Motors and the Du Pont companies. In 1923, in order to give the executives of General Motors a greater interest in their work, we organized the Managers Securities Company, made up of eighty senior and junior executives. This company bought General Motors common stock to the then market value of thirty-three million dollars. The executives paid five million dollars in cash and borrowed twenty-eight million dollars. The stockholders of the Managers Securities Company are not stockholders of General Motors. They own stock in a company which owns stock in General Motors, so that, as far as General Motors is concerned, the stock is voted as a block according to the instructions of the directors of the Managers Securities Company. This supplies an important interest which can exercise a large influence in shaping the policies of General Motors.

From $25,000 to a Million

THE holdings of the members in the securities company are adjusted in cases of men leaving the employ of the company. The plan of the Managers Securities Company contemplates no dissolution of that company, so that its holdings of General Motors stock will always be *en bloc*. The plan has been enormously successful, and much of the success of the General Motors Corporation has been due to the executives' having full responsibility and receiving financial rewards commensurate with that responsibility.

The participation in the Managers Securities Company was arranged in accordance with the position and salary of the executive. Minimum participation required a cash payment of twenty-five thousand dollars when the Managers Securities Company was organized. That minimum participation is now worth more than one million dollars.

Recently I have been advocating the formation of an equity securities corporation; that is, a corporation that will invest in common stocks only under proper and careful supervision. This company will buy the common stocks of first-class industrial corporations and issue its own stock certificates against them. This stock will be offered from time to time at a price to correspond exactly with the value of the assets of the corporation and all profit will go to the stockholders. The directors will be men of outstanding character, reputation and integrity. At regular intervals—say quarterly—the whole financial record of the corporation will be published together with all of its holdings and the cost thereof. The corporation will be owned by the public and with every transaction public. I am not at all interested in a private investment trust. The company would not be permitted to borrow money or go into any debt.

In addition to this company, there should be organized a discount company on the same lines as the finance companies

(Continued on Page 36)

1928, the same number it still contains today. Automotive companies like Nash, Chrysler, and Mack Trucks were added to the Dow, showing how manufacturing companies were on the rise.

During the 1920s, Wall Street folklore started to develop more strongly than at any other time in the past. The decade of excess was born. Magazine articles appeared, extolling the virtues of getting rich quick. It became the American thing to do. Get-rich-quick schemes were widespread, aided and abetted by many articles that appeared in newspapers and magazines describing how easy it was to make a fortune. Books appeared claiming to show the finer details of speculation to the average investor. Wall Street even became the topic of some Hollywood B movies, using the exchanges as the background for stories of love and greed. Wall Street became solidly entrenched in the popular imagination. If there were any cautionary tales in them, they went unnoticed.

The stories coming from Wall Street would have made anyone envious. Tales of great wealth being amassed in little time lured many into thinking that the streets were paved with gold. In reality, bucket shops still existed and the traders on the floor of the exchanges were still up to their old tricks. It was they who were making money while the small investor still found the road to riches strewn with stumbling blocks. Those who were accumulating the great fortunes had substantial help in manipulating prices to their own benefit.

One of the apparent great success stories of the decades was that of Billy Durant, the automobile magnate turned stock market speculator. Previously the founder of General Motors, he was forced out of the company in the early twenties and took up stock market speculation. With the help of many well-known traders on the NYSE, he assembled an investment group (called a "pool") and allegedly turned a profit of $100 million in a few years. His name became a legend in market circles, and his reputation only added fuel to the idea that anyone could become rich.

The professional traders made a fortune during the 1920s, using the pools to manipulate the prices of many stocks. They formed the

"Is Their a Market Price for Love?" asks the promotional material for a B movie and novel entitled The Wolf of Wall Street, released in 1929. Using traditional notions about the predatory floor trader, the billboard goes on to describe the film as the story behind "the ruthless fighter roaring into battle and loving it! While at home, waits the enticing beauty on whom he lavishes his wealth." The real question is: "Is she alone?"

The tale of the tape. In the Wolf of Wall Street, preoccupation with the ticker tape appears to be a mind- (and eye-) boggling affair. Brokers check the tape for daily prices.

Motor Magnates Lunching together at Thompson's 59th St. Restaurant in New York.
W. C. Durant, head of Durant Enterprises, and J. D. Dort, president of Dort Motor Car Company, former business partners.
Their fare—Ham and Beans.

One of Wall Street's best known speculators in the 1920s was Billy Durant (left). Here, he is lunching with a colleague, J. D. Dort of the Dort Motor Company. After losing control at General Motors, Durant founded Durant Motors, which was, for a time, a successful car company. But his real love was market speculation, and he helped form several pools that reportedly made a fortune. He eventually lost most of the fortune as well as the car company. In the 1920s, dozens of companies produced cars. However, none did it as successfully as Ford and General Motors, and eventually most dropped out of the business. Durant himself warned President Hoover about what he foresaw as the coming Crash, but to no avail. The market collapsed on October 24, 1929.

groups with the avowed purpose of running up (or down) the price of a stock. Many of them became subjects of adulation themselves. The pools they formed included some very well-known public figures, who were included because of their fame and connections, not their investment expertise. Small investors tried to follow the market as best they could. Fortune-tellers did a brisk business attempting to guess the market's future movements.

By 1926, the turmoil of the war years had finally faded, and the financial world was no longer the symbol of the excesses of capitalism. All

EVERYONE INTO THE POOL

A large investment pool was organized in 1928 to run up the price of RCA stock. It was instigated by the specialist in the stock, Michael Meehan, who took subscriptions from his close friends and their wives. He raised $12 million, $1 million from one investor alone. Within a few weeks, the stock had risen substantially, and the pool netted $5 million for its efforts.

*I*n the 1920s, stock gurus called "tipsters" were often employed to help investors choose a stock. Alfred T. Moore (above), president of his own tipping bureau, claimed to have given information to the son of a government official that reputedly earned almost $800,000 in 1923.

OPPOSITE

*I*n the spirit of celebration, Wall Street held another ticker tape parade, this time for the crew of the Graf Zeppelin when the dirigible made a voyage to New York from Germany in 1929.

The "corner," at Broad and Wall, outside the offices of J. P. Morgan & Co., witnessed one of Wall Street's greatest tragedies in 1921 when a massive bomb went off, causing injuries and death. The perpetrators were never apprehended.

the intense interest in investments made Wall Street something of a tourist attraction. The bull market began to draw crowds of tourists from as far away as California, and they lined the street to see their broker heroes come to work in the morning and applaud them. Five years before, that was not such a safe place to be. As recently as 1921, a bomb went off at the corner of Wall and Broad, outside the offices of J. P. Morgan & Co., causing death and injury.

Wall Street branched out and went sailing on the high seas. A famous floor trader named Michael Meehan, one of the decade's most adroit pool operators, persuaded Cunard Lines to open brokerage facilities on its trans-Atlantic ships. The company quickly agreed, and passengers were able to execute orders while sailing.

Wall Street began to look distinctly shaky in March 1929, and the Federal Reserve became disturbed about stock price levels. Charles Mitchell, the head of National City Bank, stepped in to help by adding some of his bank's funds to the market and a catastrophe was averted. But not for long. After a fairly quiet summer when even more tourists poured into New York to visit Wall Street, stock prices began to fall.

Finally, the bubble burst on October 24, 1929. As the country would soon discover, many people bought stocks using borrowed money. Even large-scale investors dealt in stocks as if they were using a bucket shop for a broker. For example, Durant's alleged profit was also accompanied by a huge debt he had amassed by buying stocks on credit. As British Chancellor of the Exchequer Winston Churchill watched from the visitor's gallery, the NYSE lost almost 12 percent of its value on turnover of almost 12 million shares, a record. The selling activity continued for a few days and then was followed by a few odd days of upward momentum. But by the end of the year, the Dow 30 had lost one-third of its value. Unfortunately, the worst was still to come. The Great Depression was already at hand, although on the surface it seemed that just another routine panic had occurred.

The immediate reaction on the Street and in the press was that Wall Street was having a bad quarter but that things would get better. Unfortunately, they did not. Banks began to fail, and personal bankruptcies were on the increase. Only a small percentage of the population actually had brokerage accounts, but many of them were especially hard hit. Much of the hot air began to fizzle out of inflated asset values. The early 1930s would see some of Wall Street's darkest hours.

Many financiers believed that the market was due to fall in the late 1920s and began warning their colleagues on the Street of what they thought was impending doom. One of the best known was Bernard Baruch, who tried in vain to assemble brokers and bankers to prevent a catastrophe. He even pledged several million dollars of his own to form a stabilization fund but was ignored. Along with Joseph P. Kennedy, another well known speculator, Baruch was out of the market when the Crash eventually occurred.

The World

FINAL NEWS EDITION

W YORK, FRIDAY, OCTOBER 25, 1929.   IN TWO SECTIONS SECTION ONE   ★★★★★★ TWO CENTS   In Greater New York | THREE CENTS Within 200 Miles | FOUR C Elsewh

ALIAN ASSASSIN MISSES HUMBERT N BELGIAN CAPITAL

tack at Tomb of Unknown Soldier on Day of Betrothal Stirs Two Nations

LY DEMANDS ACTION GAINST EXILED PLOTTERS

nce Calm, His Fiancee Overcome by Emotion, Sobs in His Arms

Special Cable to The World

RUSSELS, Oct. 24.—Crown Prince mbert, heir to the Italian throne, rowly escaped death by a political ssin's bullet here this morning, the on which he was one of the central figures in the public celebration of betrothal to Princess Marie Jose of lium.

he shot which might have ended life of the Prince of Piedmont on anniversary his parents' marriage fired at point-blank range of fif feet by Fernando di Rosa, one of own countrymen, an anti-Fascist th of twenty-one, as the scion of house of Savoy was paying tribute Belgium's Unknown Soldier. It went because the quick hand of a motor policeman struck down the would assassin's arm in the nick of time two detectives were upon him be he could shoot again.

Brussels Outraged

russels was outraged by the attpt on the Prince's life. It also ght immediate political repercus s in Italy, when demands were e for extradition of Di Rosa and sures against other plotters against Fascist regime. But the Prince re ned calm, becoming the popular o of two nations—Belgium and y—by insisting upon going on with ceremony which so nearly ended in dy.

ll's well that ends well," was his ling comment to the Count de queville, Belgian Minister of War, le the police were hurrying off Di a to prevent his lynching by an in ated public.

rincess Marie Jose was unable to rain her relief over her fiance's pe from death. Sobbing with kfulness she threw herself into the ce's arms as soon as she could n his side after the attempt on his

heir meeting took place on the steps he Italian Embassy here, which still pe the marks of recent anti-Fascist ing Careless of the eyes of the ering crowds that had followed the there from the grave of the Un wn Soldier she rushed up to him.

Market in Panic as Stocks Are Dumped in 12,894,600 Share Day; Bankers Halt I

Federal Reserve Board Meets, With Secretary Mellon Sitting In, but Announces No Action—Rumors of Rate Cut

TREASURY, HOWEVER, FINDS BASIC CONDITIONS SOUND

Senators Renew Cries in Chorus for Sweeping Investigation of Wall Street Tactics

By Elliott Thurston

Special Despatch to The World

WASHINGTON, Oct. 24.—Reassurances from the Treasury that underlying business conditions are sound as extended but unproductive meeting of the Federal Reserve Board attended by Secretary of the Treasury Mellon, and renewed cries from Capitol Hill for a sweeping investigation of Wall Street, came rapidly in the wake of the stock market debacle.

There were signs that when Secretary Mellon did the rather unusual thing of sitting in with the Federal Reserve Board at a meeting that began when the market closed and lasted for nearly two hours, some sort of statement was to be issued. Gov. Young emerged at the end of the meeting holding what seemed to be the statement, but if it was it had been vetoed. Nothing was said or intimated. The board kept its customary complete silence.

Rumors of Rate Cut

Rumors were going around that the rediscount rate might be cut back to 5 per cent., after the sudden full point advance that was intended but failed to halt the upward march of the market. Another rumor was that the board might announce credit would be available at tight points, if needed. This was meant to give a reassuring psychological effect like that produced in Florida by a similar announcement that halted the closing of banks there.

The Treasury preserved an unshaken front of confidence, ascribed the latest cyclonic effects to technicalities, which appeared to include bear raiding, and heavily stressed the point that business is sound, and that even the worst spots, coal and textiles, have touched bottom and are on the upgrade.

Talk of Tax Cut

The tone of optimism was so strong that the high official who commented

Outside J. P. Morgan & Co.'s

By World Staff Photographer

Scene at Broad and Wall Streets During Stock Market Excitement. Insets Show THOMAS W. LAMONT, Morgan Partner (Left), and CHARLES E. MITCHELL, National City Chairman (Right), Who Turned the Tide of Selling

BUSINESS IS SAFE, FINANCIERS ASSERT

Leaders See No Economic Basis in Securities Panic

"Considering the record-breaking earnings in many industries," said Lewis E. Pierson, Chairman of the Board of the Irving Trust Company, last night, in commenting on the break in prices yesterday "we may well re

MEN ON EXCHANGE KEEP THEIR NERVE

In Face of Disaster, They Joke Amid Violent Scene

By Kenneth Campbell

The men of the Stock Exchange kept their nerve yesterday when the impending wave of financial disaster made the barricades of their money and cunning creak and totter and

Richard Whitney's Cry of for Steel" Halts Decline Record Day's Disorder on Stock Exchange

EXPERTS TERM COLLAPS SPECULATIVE PHENOME

Effect Is Felt on the Curb Throughout Nation—Fina cial District Goes Wild

By Laurence Stern

The stock markets of the co tottered on the brink of panic ye day as a prosperous people, gone denly hysterical with fear, atten simultaneously to sell a record-b ing volume of securities for whe they would bring.

The result was a financial n mare, comparable to nothing eve fore experienced in Wall Stree rocked the financial district t foundations, hopelessly overwh its mechanical facilities, chille blood with terror.

In a society built largely on dence, with real wealth expressed or less inaccurately by pieces of the entire fabric of economic str threatened to come toppling dow

Into the frantic hands of a tho brokers on the floor of the New Stock Exchange poured the sellin ders of the world. It was sell, se —hour after desperate hour unt P. M.

The Tide Is Turned

Then, in as dramatic a manoeu financial history has ever know tide was magically turned by th ganized power of the city's l banking interests.

With prices at their worst a buzz of rumors turning ordinarily men silly, a quiet group of fina gathered in the austere offices P. Morgan & Co., at Wall and Streets. They included Thomas mont, Thomas Cochrane and Morgan partners; Charles E. Mi Chairman of the National City Albert H. Wiggin, Chairman o Chase National Bank; W. C. P President of the Guaranty Trust pany, and others.

No formal statement was issue writing newspaper men Mr. La spoke words of reassurance dignified and restrained, expressi

A headline from the "day after," October 25, 1929. Everyone assumed that the bankers' $130 million pool of funds put together by Morgan and the other major banks would be enough to stabilize the market, but that was not the case. The market quickly resumed its downward trend, and by the end of the year the Dow 30 stood at 238, down from a high of 351. It would move even lower in the 1930s.

Losing it all. A small speculator attempts to sell his car in order to pay his margin debt. The Crash forced the liquidation of many small investors' positions because they could not pay their brokers the money they owed on their margin. The brokers would then sell the stocks in order to recoup some of the money, and the market would fall even further as a result. That sort of problem would be remedied in the 1930s when new regulations appeared governing margin trading.

SOUND ADVICE

Bernard Baruch was one of many well known speculators who decided to get out of the market before the 1929 Crash occurred. He related his method for making money—and holding on to it: "Repeatedly, in my market operations I have sold a stock while it still was rising – and that is one reason why I have held on to my fortune." Like many other investors, he was dismayed by the Crash but watched it from the sidelines without losing any money.

THE ART OF
SPECULATION
CARRET

WHAT TO DO —
HOW TO DO IT

Never say die. This book, The Art of Speculation *by Philip Carret, was one of Wall Street's most popular books even though it followed the 1929 Crash. On the back cover, other similar books are also advertised, including an analysis of the market crash by economist Irving Fisher and the more practical* Watch Your Margin *by an author who demurely preferred to remain anonymous. This shows that many at the time did not believe that the Crash was actually as serious as it eventually proved to be.*

While many blue-chip stocks were bringing prices of as much as $1,500 per share, this early movie *Bottoms Up* shows stocks as cheap as $0.50 Made after the Crash, the movie features scenery that shows the world slightly askew, which was a polite way of describing the aftermath of the 1929 crash. Stocks were not as cheap as groceries, however, although they would not recover for almost a decade.

*I*n *this scene, shot outside the offices of*
Henry Clews & Co., one of Wall Street's oldest
and best known brokers, the window has no bars and
did not need any. Clews had been a broker on the Street
since the post-Civil War period and had his memoirs
published several times. The Crash of 1929 was the
worst ever experienced in terms of percentage drops
in the market, on record volume.

Popular legend gives the impression that suicides were common after the Crash. Although a few traders committed suicide after losing everything, the actual number was fairly low. That did not stop Will Rogers from telling the story about the New York hotel clerk who asked incoming guests whether they wanted a room "for sleeping or for jumping?"

THE 1930s AND 1940s

THE GOOD TIMES EXPERIENCED DURING the 1920s were only a memory as the new decade began. The Jazz Age stopped so abruptly that it seemed as if someone had suddenly turned off the phonograph. Wall Street did not feel the full brunt of the economic downturn immediately, but the force of it was building quickly.

The Crash began to have serious effects within a year. The decade of the 1930s would be remembered as one of slow economic growth, high unemployment, and a general pessimism about the future. Some of Wall Street's most significant moments occurred during the 1930s as the country tried to come to grips with the financial community it blamed for many of the problems.

The 1930s began on a sour note as bank crashes became common. Many had lent money to margin traders and failed when the loans were not repaid. Others failed because of bad or fraudulent management. The property boom of the 1920s ended abruptly as well, leaving banks with mountains of unpaid debt. Without deposit insurance, customers began to withdraw their money, causing severe credit problems that only compounded the economic crisis. Faith in the financial system crumbled quickly. Going door-to-door begging for food became common as once proud workers lost their life savings.

OPPOSITE

What's the stink? A tear gas cylinder, placed in the ventilation system of the NYSE, forced traders onto the corner of Broad and Wall in August 1933.

Then Wall Street became embroiled in one of the nastiest episodes in its history. Although many on the Street continued to believe that the Crash was not as serious as it eventually proved to be, traders on the exchanges were busy selling short many stocks that they knew would fall in price as the Depression deepened. They were making money in a falling market while unemployment rose to new highs and the country sank into dire economic straits. Traders on the commodities markets were doing the same as commodity prices fell sharply. Soon their secret leaked to the outside world.

President Hoover reacted angrily to the disturbing trend by calling for an investigation. The "bear hunt" officially had begun. Those who were profiting from the country's declining economic fortunes were singled out for reproach. The government launched investigations into the practices of short sellers and examined lists of those who participated. The NYSE steadfastly maintained that short selling did no harm to the econ-

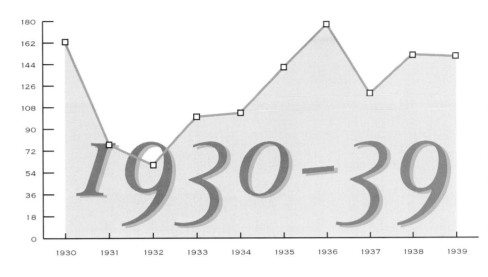

omy, but its denials were ignored. The behavior of traders *after* the Crash was more despicable than the behavior that led to it in the first place.

After Franklin D. Roosevelt won the 1932 presidential election, the investigation was given new focus. The Senate was questioning Wall Street again after twenty years. The Senate hearings proved to be the most sensational in the Street's history. The long list of bankers and brokers who were called ranged from J. P. Morgan, Jr., and Charles Mitchell to the powerful floor traders who organized the pools in the 1920s. Their revelations proved to be embarrassing for them and their associates. Wall Street's public relations nightmare had begun.

The congressional hearings lasted for months and exposed the once secret side of Wall Street. Top brokers and bankers were questioned about their

A commodities futures broker checks the tape for prices. Futures brokers were selling many contracts short, profiting as agricultural prices fell during the Depression. They would escape the regulations that Wall Street was forced to endure in 1933 and 1934.

The alleged "bear list" of those accused of selling short on the NYSE while prices were falling dramatically and the economy was falling into the Great Depression is examined by officials of the exchange, including NYSE president Richard Whitney (center).

Members of the Senate Banking Committee investigate the stock market. Senators Carey of Wyoming and Blaine of Wisconsin question Mathew Brush, a prominant operator, about his activities selling stocks short after the 1929 Crash.

J. P. "Jack" Morgan and his son Junius (leaning) listen to the proceedings of the Pecora hearings investigating the stock market and financial practices, in May 1933. Morgan was the star witness for the committee, which interviewed dozens of Wall Street bankers, brokers, and traders.

M̲organ *(center left) listens to committee chief counsel Ferdinand Pecora (papers in hand) as he testified during the hearings in Washington. Morgan admitted that he had not paid income tax for the previous three years.*

In a lighter moment, Jack Morgan (right) jokes with an onlooker at the hearings while Ferdinand Pecora (second from left) watches. In the center, wearing a hat, is Senator Carter Glass of Virginia, one of the authors of the famous Glass-Steagall Act, passed in 1933, that separated commercial and investment banking. When the act was passed, Morgan eventually chose the banking business and spun his securities business off to the newly formed Morgan Stanley & Co.

Another star witness at the Senate hearings was Harold Stuart (left), president of Halsey, Stuart & Co. Stuart testified about the fall of a huge Chicago utilities company during the Depression.

The empty NYSE board room before a trading day began.

prices collapsed. Herbert Hoover's presidency came to an end as well. When FDR took office in March 1933, sweeping changes occurred almost overnight.

In March 1933, Roosevelt ordered a banking holiday to sort out the nation's banking mess. Congress passed the Securities Act in 1933, the first of its kind ever passed on a federal level. Investment bankers were not pleased since the law required all companies coming to market to register their securities. Then in 1934 Congress passed the law the Street most dreaded, the Securities Exchange Act. The newly formed Securities and Exchange Commission (SEC) was now the regulator of the stock markets and dictated practices that were to be used in trading. Even though Prohibition was repealed a year earlier, no one on the

Street felt like celebrating. The only ray of light was that Joseph P. Kennedy (father of the future president), one of Wall Street's best known operators of the 1920s, was named SEC chairman.

Reform of Wall Street and the banks was a continuing priority of the New Deal even after the momentous legislation passed in 1933 and 1934. Many new investment banks were created in 1934. Banks had to choose which side of the business they wanted to pursue, and many newly spun-off investment banks were created by those that eschewed the securities business. The SEC continued to press the NYSE for reforms, and the investment bankers remained hostile to the Securities Act, regarding it as a government intrusion into private enterprise.

The market remained depressed until 1935 when it began to slowly rise. During that time, Congress passed some of the most important legislation of the century, including the Social Security Act.

> **W**illiam O. Douglas was no friend of Wall Street. While an SEC commissioner, he described investment bankers as "financial termites . . . who practice the art of predatory or high finance. They destroy the legitimate function of finance and become a common enemy of investors and business." Douglas pressed Wall Street into reforms in the 1930s.

William O. Douglas was one of Wall Street's severest critics in the 1930s. As SEC commissioner he often attacked the Street's practices and commission rates. FDR later nominated him to the Supreme Court.

After the Glass-Steagall Act was passed, many new investment banks were created. The best known was Morgan Stanley, named after Henry S. Morgan, a son of Jack Morgan, and Harold Stanley, its first chairman. Both were former J. P. Morgan & Co. employees. The new investment bank shared back room operations with its former parent for a short period. Others created included the First Boston Corp., Harriman, Ripley, and the Union Securities Corp. Chase Manhattan and National City also shed their securities affiliates.

Henry S. Morgan, Jack's son, became the head of the new investment banking company spun off by the bank in 1934. He and Harold Stanley, a former Morgan employee, were partners at the new firm, which picked up all the bank's former investment banking clients.

B rokers had little to cheer about in the early 1930s. The market started to rise from its lows in early 1935, and floor traders gathered outside the NYSE for a group picture to celebrate what they thought was the end of the bear market.

B usiness for brokers was better for the first half of 1937 before the market dropped again, back to the
125 level on the Dow. Here, brokers talk to clients by phone. They have megaphones on their desks so
that they can shout orders to clerks.

OPPOSITE

A ctivity began to pick up on the NYSE in 1936 as hopes for an end
to the Depression began to rise. This is a scene of the floor in 1936,
busy but not as frenzied as in the 1920s.

After a particularly busy day, a worker cleans up the exchange floor. The 1937 market drop disappointed many who thought that the New Deal's economic policies would be more successful.

The Dow crept slowly back up in 1938, and an enterprising street vendor decided to sell suspenders to floor traders outside the side entrance to the exchange. "I heard the market was holding up," he said, "and I figured that pants needed securities like anything else. Besides, remember these guys lost their shirts in 1929 and maybe these things will come in handy."

The newly created SEC continually pressed Wall Street for reforms. It put pressure on member firms on the Street to organize, and they responded by forming a trade group that was eventually called the National Association of Securities Dealers, officially recognized when Congress passed the Maloney Act in 1937. Wall Street now had its first federally recognized organization in the NASD, the name given to the unlisted over-the-counter market.

Despite the progress, 1937 proved to be a bad year. The market dropped over a hundred points by early 1938, and questions were being

The first meeting of the Board of Governors of the NYSE after reforms were implemented in 1937 at the behest of William O. Douglas and the SEC. William McChesney Martin became the first paid full-time president of the NYSE.

asked again about the health of the economy and the future of the Street. The market added insult to injury since the old bear market still persisted after seven years. And the tricks of the old traders were no longer tolerated. Several had been barred from the exchange and prosecuted for their activities following the Crash. The former president of the NYSE would soon be discovered to have embezzled from the exchange's funds and would be sent to prison. Wall Street's once prominent stars had quickly receded from view. Wall Street had gone from being the jewel in the crown of the economy to the dark dungeon of fraud and deceit.

An assistant attorney general conducts a hearing into the affairs of Richard Whitney & Co., one of Wall Street's better known firms in the 1920s and 1930s. Its senior partner, Richard Whitney, president of the NYSE from 1930 to 1935, was found to have embezzled $1 million from a NYSE fund. The firm was forced to close in 1938, and Whitney was sentenced to a prison term in Sing Sing. He was the only NYSE president ever jailed.

Further reform was in the works. The NYSE instituted changes that took it out of the hands of part-time chairmen who were presidents of brokerage houses and put it in the hands of a full-time president who was committed to reform. Its board also began to meet more regularly; and while it was still an exclusive group, it was no longer the old boys' club it had once been before the Crash. As the decade came to a close, big business and the New Deal were still very much at loggerheads,

After serving almost 3½ years of his prison term, Richard Whitney was released from Sing Sing in 1941. After leaving prison, he went to Barnstable, Massachusetts, to superintend a dairy farm.

with many in the administration feeling that Wall Street and big business together were responsible for both the Crash and the inability of the economy to pull itself out of the Depression.

In the 1940s, the bear went into hibernation but the bull hardly showed its head. War broke out in Europe in 1939. Antiwar sentiment kept the United States neutral, but the Roosevelt administration began plans for aiding the Allies and for eventually involving the United States. For the last seven years the Roosevelt administration had been publicly bashing industry, but it realized that it now needed industry as an ally if the United States was to become involved in the war. But did it need Wall Street?

*D*uring the war, women became valuable employees on the Street, filling in for men serving in the armed forces. Here, the woman standing receives an order from the floor and passes it to a typist who officially records it.

W omen were also employed as telephonists (operators) and guides on the exchanges.
The two women here proudly display their official NYSE jackets.

professional allegiances checked to determine whether they had been acting as a monopoly. When the suit was finally thrown out of court, Wall Street was exonerated of wrongdoing and could concentrate on the bull market that was about to begin. After more than twenty years of depression and war, the economy was poised for new challenges.

A fter the war ended, brokerage was becoming respectable again as economic conditions began to improve. Here, a popular stage star, Irene Bordoni, visits with her broker W. D. Hutton of Hutton & Co. at his new branch offices on West 57th Street in Manhattan. She was his first customer.

OVERLEAF

A fter the war ended, women remained working at the exchange. In this photo taken in 1947, women in the central tube room relay prices to member firms' offices around the country.

4

THE 1950s AND 1960s

THE 1950S AND 1960S WERE DECADES OF transition for Wall Street. After more than twenty years of turmoil, the country was poised for better times and the Street was poised for a bull market. The last genuine bull market had occurred before the 1929 Crash during the giddy 1920s when borrowing money for speculation was common. When the Korean War ended, an enormous pent-up demand exploded for consumer goods, new homes, and even stocks. Wall Street had something to smile about for the first time in decades.

Politics also smiled upon the Street. A Republican was in the White House for the first time since 1932. Eisenhower symbolized his era — a war hero who triumphantly entered politics with tremendous popular support. The political climate encouraged growth, and that became the dominant theme for investing for the next twenty years. The stock market bid up the price of companies that demonstrated earnings growth, and many new concepts appeared that employed the idea of constant expansion in their strategies. While the bull market of the 1920s was a speculative bubble, that of the 1950s would be supported by strong fundamentals.

Investing also became popular with middle-class investors for the first time in a generation. Memories of the Crash and the bank failures

OPPOSITE

Wall Street throws another ticker tape parade early in the decade. General Douglas MacArthur is honored in 1951.

OPPOSITE

An exterior shot of the old New York Curb Exchange at its Trinity Place location.

LEFT

The McCormicks ring the bell on the last official trading day of the old Curb Exchange before it changed its name.

The Curb Exchange officially changed its name to the American Stock Exchange on January 5, 1953.

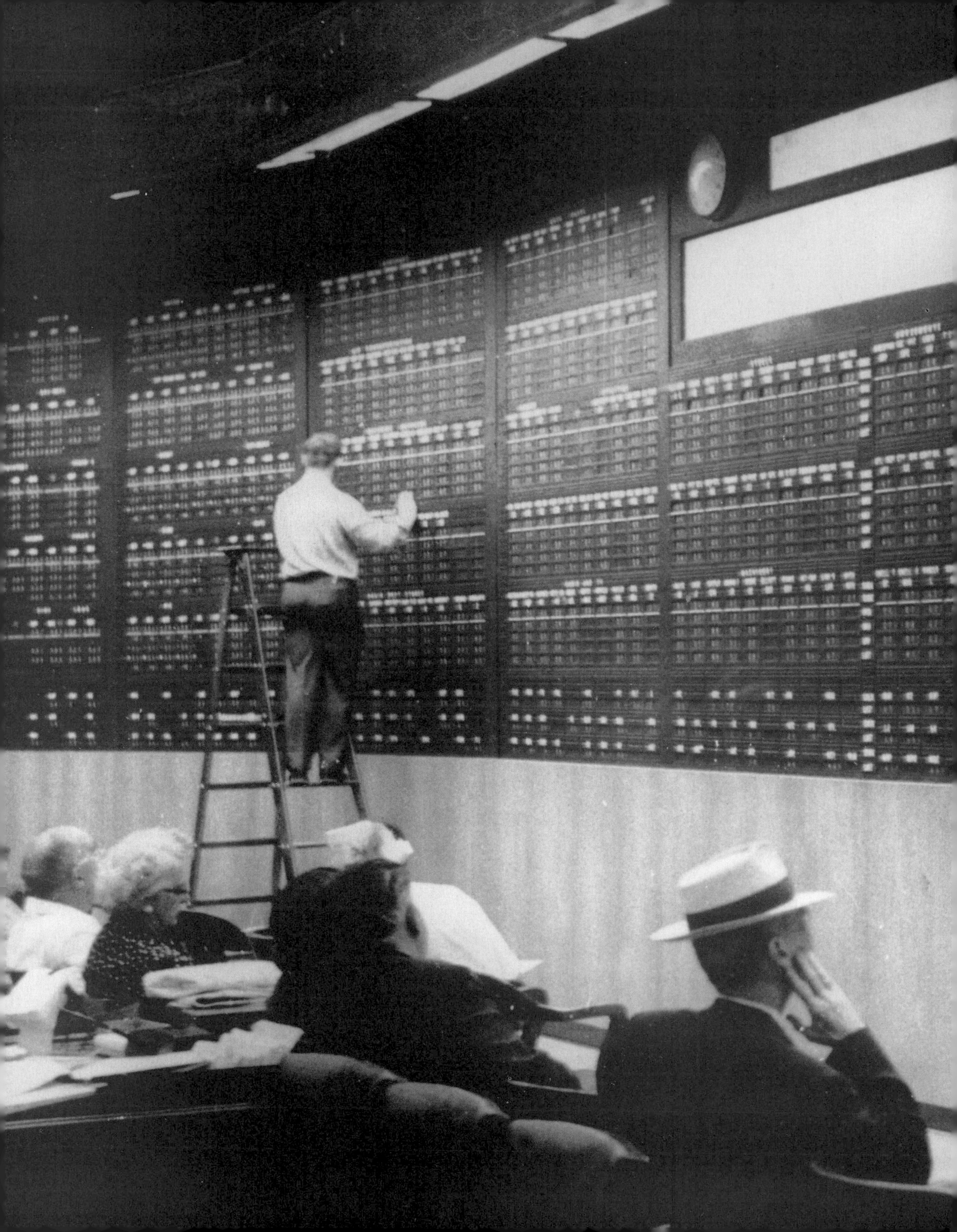

B rokers began to open
more branch offices
in the 1950s to reach a
growing population eager
to invest. Here, investors
watch the electronic
quotations board at a
Bache & Co. office
in Chicago.

market but still wanted to participate in the country's growth. Shareholder activism began to develop. Shareholders large and small started to ask how their companies were making money and occasionally raised social concerns as well. Annual meetings would no longer be quiet affairs between a company and its institutional shareholders. Small investors began to assert themselves as never before.

The 1950s were not quite the halcyon sitcom years portrayed on television and in other popular media. The cold war appeared in full force. When the Russians beat the Americans into space by launching *Sputnik* in 1957, the country was shocked. New technologies made the prospect of global war more possible than the more conventional wars fought in the past, and stock in companies that produced cutting-edge armaments and materiels was in

A member of the League of Women Stockholders uses a portable p.a. system to address a crowd in 1958 at the General Motors shareholders' meeting.

Shareholder activism began to increase in the 1950s. Here, a woman who held one share of RCA stock waves her finger to make a point at the annual shareholders' meeting.

The floor of the NYSE after the Federal Reserve announced a drop in margin rates from 70 to 50 percent, a level at which it has remained since. The action sent the market higher.

In the 1950s, food and drink were banned from the floor of the NYSE. A trader's son-in-law worked for him on the floor, buying and selling shares of Coca-Cola, among other stocks. One day, the young man sneaked a can of Coke onto the floor so that he could quench his thirst during a quiet moment. When the senior trader saw the open can, he ordered the young man to get rid of the Coke. Doing as he was told, the young trader sold all the Coke shares the senior trader owned, costing his father-in-law a loss of $90,000.

the most demand. Defense contractors became the most sought-after companies in the market. Anything that had to do with space or war quickly became investor favorites.

A new form of company arose that sought to capitalize on the trend. Massive new corporations were being formed by a new breed of corporate leader who came from outside the established main line of American industrialists. This new breed of chief executive was committed to assembling a vast, disparate array of companies under one corporate roof called the conglomerate. While the conglomerates were widely diversified, their chief preoccupation was defense. They were the main contractors to the military and became part of the hotly debated military-industrial complex that dominated Wall Street and the defense establishment between the Korean War and the mid-1970s.

The stock market picked up momentum after the Korean War, and the averages began to rise in 1954. The Dow Jones Industrial Average would almost triple in value during the 1950s. The increase was very orderly, with no major spikes to the averages despite Eisenhower's 1955 heart attack and two recessions that temporarily set the market back. The enormous growth unlocked by increased production, based upon renewed consumer spending, helped many stocks rise. America was in the process of becoming suburbanized, and consumers spent more on housing, automobiles, and other consumer durables than ever before. The national highway system was begun, making the automobile even more of a necessity than it was before. Automobile manufacturers, defense contractors, computer companies, and pharmaceutical and technology companies became the new blue chips, replacing the wheelhorses of the previous decades.

But when compared with the 1960s, the 1950s were tame indeed and would rightly take their place as a nostalgic decade when things seemed fairly placid. The 1960s were years of great scientific and technological innovation, political upheaval, and assassination. On Wall Street, they were years of great volatility. The stock market began a slow climb toward the 1,000 level but never made the milestone. Most signif-

As brokerages became larger, brokers were moved farther away from the ticker tape. Here, a broker uses binoculars to see the tape from his desk.

The first Mexican bond was sold in New York in 1963. Here, Mexican finance officials confer with investment bankers from Kuhn Loeb, the lead manager.

icantly, the market took several sharp plunges during the decade that made investors increasingly wary of the effects that these events could have on the markets.

The decade of the 1960s witnessed the birth of the modern merger and acquisition business on Wall Street. Helping conglomerates accumulate companies became a major source of profits for many firms. Mergers grew at their strongest rate since the 1920s. Many well-known companies became the targets of the conglomerates, and the "hostile bid" became a popular method of acquiring an unsuspecting company. The conglomerates were often painted as hostile acquirers, "gunslingers" out to shoot down even established companies if the price was right. The characterization was often correct.

Another almost forgotten factor reared its head during the 1960s— inflation. Inflation caused by the war in Vietnam began to rise and adversely affect the markets. It affected stock and bond returns and made investors nervous. Investor activism also continued. Taking a cue from political activists, investors began to more openly question companies than in the past. And there were many more investors in the market. Main Street and Wall Street were closer than at any time before.

Building upon the foundations established in the 1950s, Wall Street opened more brokerage offices around the country, bringing more and more investment products to Main Street. Interest in mutual funds continued, and increasingly more people began speculating in the market. But unlike the 1920s, many of the investment advisers were using solid investment information rather than "tips." The tipster had given way to the equity analyst. Tips based upon inside information were now illegal.

Wall Street fondly called the 1960s the "go-go years." Companies that emphasized growth quickly became investment favorites, and their stock prices soared. Conglomerates were at the top of the list, registering prices that had not been seen since the 1920s. Many of the conglomerates became household names, and their chief executive officers became popular figures with the media. Many ventured outside their established lines of business with disastrous results. Companies in all sorts of businesses finally fizzled as the market realized they were cumbersome and did not live up to expectations.

Toward the end of the decade, Wall Street began to feel the crunch of overexpansion. Several well-publicized scandals broke out over the financial results of some of the growth companies. And then the Street

The market became very nervous in 1962 as President Kennedy dealt with the steel industry crisis. Here, brokers in a midtown office in Manhattan watch the tape and newswires closely.

Many conglomerateurs of the 1960s were not main-line Wall Streeters but those relatively new to the business of acquisitions who succeeded despite their early lack of connections and experience with the Wall Street establishment. The head of the Rapid American Corporation, Menshulem Riklis, emigrated to the United States from Israel with his parents at an early age. Harold Geneen of ITT, was a clerk on Wall Street when he was in his teens and James Ling of LTV started his acquisitions career as an electrical supplier.

Business increased at a rapid rate in the 1960s as the indices rose. Here, in the back room of its New York headquarters, Merrill Lynch employs shredding equipment to obliterate the paper records once they had been officially transcribed. The machine was nicknamed "the hurricane."

Customers watch the tape from behind a partition in a brokerage office in New York in 1965, a time when the market had become very volatile.

DOW JONES INDUSTRIAL AVERAGE, *1960-69*

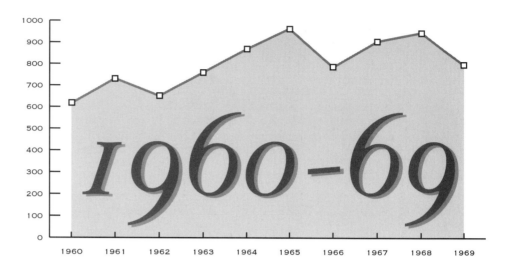

Robert Haack, the president of the NYSE, opens a session. With him on the podium is Gustave Levy, chairman of the NYSE board. Haack openly advocated reforms for the NYSE, many of which were implemented some years later.

itself suffered its own problems when the sheer volume of paperwork put several member firms under strain. The exchanges had to proclaim "holidays" on otherwise normal business days in order to cope with the record-keeping mess. By the end of the decade, more than 150 firms had failed, showing that the Street was as vulnerable as its customers.

Despite the signs of strain, there was still much to cheer. Work began on the World Trade Center towers that would eventually house many Wall Street firms and commodity brokers and exchanges. The occasional ticker tape parade was still held. And in the eighteen-years period between the return of General MacArthur during the Korean War and the late 1960s, the celebrations now ranged from honoring war heroes to welcoming astronauts back from space.

Wall Street was on the verge of some of its

most momentous changes since the 1930s. But this time, the changes were to come from within, rather than being imposed from the outside. The days of relatively small member firms, run as partnerships, were quickly to become a thing of the past. Large brokers would replace them as the idea of the financial department store began to make a comeback for the first time since the 1920s. Many member firms made plans to go public, selling shares to investors for the first time. The 1920s were not totally forgotten. Some of the developments of forty years before still seemed like a good idea during the go-go years. But implementing them would be difficult because the second great bear market of the century was just around the corner.

The floor of the NYSE as it records the busiest day in its history on April 3, 1968. Until then, the record day had been October 29, 1929, when over 16 million shares traded.

Another conglomerate head, James Ling of Ling-Temco-Vaught, later the LTV Corporation, was always on the prowl for companies to merge with. Ling was very flamboyant, and like many of his fellow conglomerateurs, often overlooked details when he wanted to make an acquisition. Deciding that a bank would make a nice fit with his other companies, he asked an associate to see if the Bank of England was for sale. He was told, regrettably, that it was not.

Charles Bludhorn, the architect of Gulf & Western Industries' growth in the 1960s, took the plunge into the entertainment industry when he purchased Paramount in 1966. Here he is shown at a Paramount movie with his wife and Mrs. Edward Kennedy (left).

5

THE 1970s AND 1980s

WALL STREET HAD NOT EXPERIENCED A contrast like the one between the 1970s and 1980s since the days of the booming 1920s and the Depression. The market would unexpectedly sink to lows not seen in years. But unlike the previous bear market after 1929, there was no crash that destroyed the hopes of a generation. Still, that proved of little consolation to investors and traders.

Inflation was the main culprit behind the market's slowdown in the late 1960s and early 1970s. Yet that did not stop the market from rising to a historic high. In 1972, the "Dow hit a thou," and it seemed as if the market had finally shaken its jitters. Despite the occasion, the Dow Jones Industrial Average was still less than three times the index of October 1929, over forty years before.

Events quickly swamped the market. The OPEC price rises that began in 1973 proved to be more than just a one-time adjustment to the price of oil. In addition to the periodic oil price rises, the Vietnam War lingered and the Watergate affair put the White House under siege. Despite the political and economic chaos, the Street was moving ahead with its own expansion. In 1971, the NASD had announced the birth of its automated quotations system, NASDAQ. Now that the over-the-

OPPOSITE

The twin towers of the World Trade Center were still under construc-tion in the early 1970s. The buildings would eventually house many Wall Street offices plus several small exchanges.

counter market had become computerized, the NYSE was facing a potentially serious rival and would soon be pushed into its own reforms. Meanwhile the Dow continued to climb and appeared ready to break 1,100. And then the roof fell in.

In 1973 and 1974, the market took the second worst beating in its history when it plunged by over 50 percent. Shortly after President Nixon resigned in 1974, the Dow sank below 600. The oil embargo was in place, and the markets found little solace. The volatility did have a bright side, however. The options markets and the commodity futures

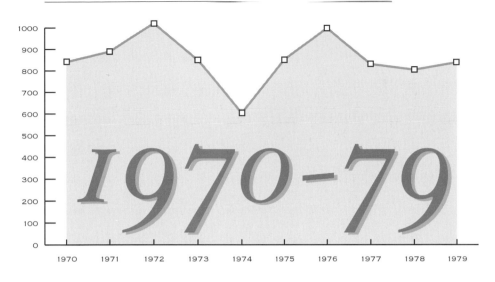

1970-79

markets in Chicago were developing options on stocks and futures on interest rate instruments that would prove vital to investors in years ahead. The wild markets were a good testing ground for these new instruments, but the stock and bond markets failed to see the bright side and continued to suffer.

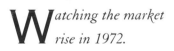

Watching the market rise in 1972.

Wall Street underwent major reforms in 1975. For years, large, institutional clients had been complaining about the commissions charged at the NYSE. Finally, on May 1, dubbed "May Day," the exchange allowed negotiated commissions in an effort to lower charges to its best customers. The new commission structure

also allowed discount brokers to flourish, offering lower rates for their retail customers. This attracted many small investors and provided incentives for them to invest in an otherwise risky investment environment.

Inflation refused to be subdued, however. Between 1975 and 1976, the Dow gained back all its lost territory only to give it up again in 1977. By the end of the decade, during the Iran hostage crisis, oil had risen to $30 per barrel, fifteen times its price in 1970. Americans became fearful of foreign influence because of the weak dollar. Wall Street was the scene of more than one demonstration against foreigners, who some thought were bent upon dominating Americans with their investments. The big oil companies were also suspected of hoarding oil in an effort to drive up its price. By the end of the tumultuous decade, inflation continued with a slowing economy. "Stagflation" was coined as the term to describe the combination of the two.

Shareholder meetings were not getting any friendlier in the 1970s. At this annual meeting of the Penn Central Railroad, a shareholder activist scuffles with another shareholder.

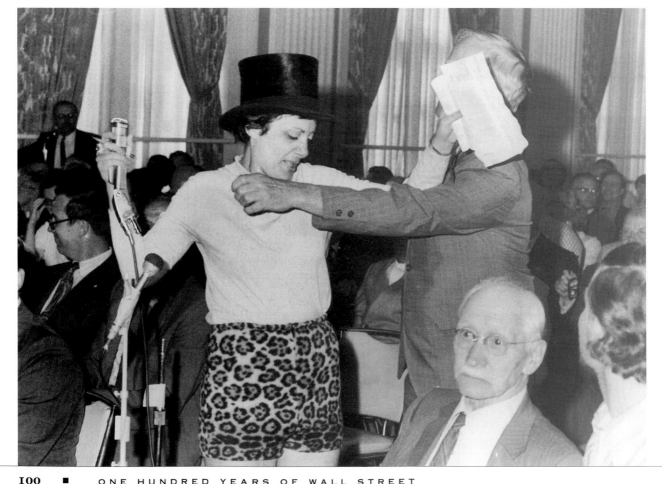

The front of Fraunces Tavern, a Wall Street landmark since the eighteenth century. Financiers had been lunching at the restaurant for over 150 years until terror struck in January 1975.

Four people were killed and forty injured at Fraunces' when a terrorist group set off a bomb.

New York City was on the financial rocks in 1975 when Wall Street firms helped the Municipal Assistance Corporation issue bonds to fend off bankruptcy.

OPPOSITE

The market happily hit a thousand again in 1976 before plunging to 750.

Workers guide a steel beam into place on the floor of the Amex in 1977. The exchange expanded by adding extra floors above the trading floor.

Brokers continued to open offices in the mid-1970s. At Merrill Lynch's booth at Grand Central Station, commuters could stop and check the prices of their favorite stocks.

A popular story on the Street concerns a trader who stayed out too late one night drinking with his colleagues. Rather than go home, he stayed at a local hotel in order to sleep it off. The next morning, he discovered his clothes were missing. Panicked, he called some of his colleagues and asked them to send over some clothes. They obliged, but instead of a normal business suit they sent a white bunny outfit. Undeterred, the trader donned the outfit and proceeded to the floor of the NYSE where he became the first known rabbit to grace the floor in almost 200 years.

Brokers check their books in 1977 as the Dow closes below 800 for the first time in more than two years. This proved to be the lowest point for the market since 1974, although the rally was still five years away.

Bernard "Bernie" Cornfeld in his New York offices on Park Avenue. Cornfeld was one of the most successful mutual fund promoters of the 1960s. His Investors Overseas Services funds were located offshore. Eventually, however, his mutual fund empire would collapse.

Wall Street was having a difficult time selling new securities in this environment. Volatile markets made investors wary, and new bonds and stocks did not always receive a warm welcome in the markets. Then in 1979, the Federal Reserve chairmanship became vacant and President Carter appointed Paul Volcker, a Wall Street favorite, to the job. The Street would suffer as Volcker's dose of monetary medicine led to higher interest rates. It would take several more years before the Street had anything to smile about.

The early 1980s became Wall Street's darkest hour since the 1930s. The market remained below 1,000 as the Fed maintained its tight monetary policy. Bond yields soared, and the country underwent major changes. The giant AT&T formally broke up in early 1984. Japanese investors discovered the Treasury bond market and made huge investments at a time when there was much suspicion concerning foreign investors. Wall Street enjoyed the business, but it was not indicative of a bull market, only opportunistic buying by a major trading partner. The bull market would be triggered by a more optimistic investment environment that was slowly building.

Several moves by the Reagan administration gave the market the impetus it needed. A cut in the capital gains tax was introduced, and the Fed's policies began to bring interest rates down. The combination provided a needed lift, and investors began to return to the market. The Dow pushed past 1,000 again in late 1982 and never looked back. The biggest bull market in history had begun.

*P*resident Carter
named Paul Volcker
as chairman of the Federal
Reserve in 1979. Volcker
was a veteran Treasury and
Fed official who had the
support of Wall Street as
he tackled inflation with a
tight monetary policy.

REAL PRIME INTEREST RATES

7.6%

3.4%

2.0%   1.8%

1.2%

70   75   80   82

*P*aul Volcker
explains his views
on inflation and the
growing budget deficit
to a congressional
committee in 1982.
It took two more years
before inflation was
under control.

Treasury Secretary Don Regan, appearing before a congressional committee in 1984, discusses the Reagan administration's budget deficits. The administration maintained that the deficits, while large, were relatively small when compared with the size of the economy.

The 1980s quickly acquired the nickname "the decade of greed." It was widely and correctly assumed that, as in the 1920s, the rich were getting richer while the poor were becoming poorer in real terms. An enormous budget deficit created cutbacks in many government services, and the number of homeless was increasing along with the number of market millionaires. One of the best examples of the antics of the new rich could be found in the junk bond market, which began producing new, low-quality corporate bond issues in the early 1980s.

One of the junk bond market's best known promotional events was held for several years running in Hollywood. Michael Milken and his cohorts at Drexel Burnham organized the annual Predator's Ball, where investment bankers, politicians, and investors came together for a few days of frolicking under the guise of discussing junk bonds. When the festivities were combined with the amount of investment banking fees that Milken and his colleagues were earning, it became clear that the new market of the 1980s was a gold mine in the investment banking sense. Milken reputedly earned over $600 million in one year, easily making him the highest-paid American ever. But the gilt came off the rose rather quickly.

Junk bonds alone did not dominate the financial news of the 1980s. Small, innovative companies were entering the market, and they would quickly come to dominate not just their markets but the entire economy. For years, Wall Street and politicians had been worried about the loss of American industrial and technological leadership. As the 1980s wore on, it became apparent that American business was on the rise again. Companies like Microsoft, Compaq, Intel, and a host of other high-tech businesses became the standard-bearers for their new industries. Their spectacular growth in the 1980s would explode in the 1990s when they became dominant in the global markets as well.

During the 1980s, two major problems confronted Wall Street and the economy. A massive trade deficit and a towering budget deficit combined to put some pressure on the markets, and Wall Street openly backed a plan to reduce the budget deficit through legislation. The NYSE continued to rise near 3,000 when whispers of an insider trading scandal began to circulate. Soon, the whispers became official when several notable investment bankers and brokers were arrested. Some were confronted at their offices and handcuffed, for the television cameras to record. One of them was arbitrageur Ivan Boesky, who used inside information in trading stocks that were involved in takeover bids. Once confronted, Boesky pointed a finger at Michael Milken.

OVERLEAF

Traders on the floor of the NYSE observe a minute of silence for the astronauts killed in the Challenger *disaster in January 1986.*

DOW JONES INDUSTRIAL AVERAGE, *1980-89*

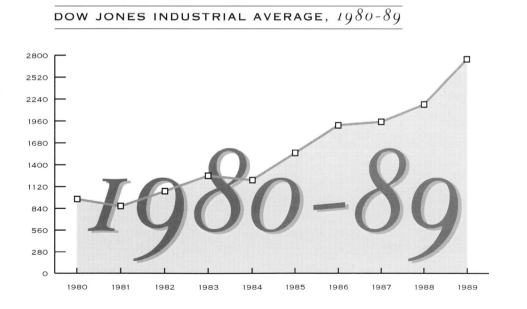

*I*van Boesky (left), the once celebrated arbitrageur, leaves a New York court ashen-faced after being sentenced to three years in prison for his part in the insider trading scandal of a year before.

Much was made of Michael Milken's compensation at Drexel Burnham Lambert. Called the highest-paid executive of all time, Milken nevertheless earned his money because of a deal he struck with Drexel that allowed his junk bond group to keep about 2 percent of the fees obtained from underwriting junk bonds. So if the firm underwrote $200 billion worth of bonds, his group kept about $4 billion for itself.

OPPOSITE

*A*s the insider trading scandals of the mid-1980s started to surface, many brokers took refuge at Harry's, Wall Street's best known after-hours watering hole.

The merger and acquisition business on the Street was recording deals at a record pace. The junk bond market helped finance many of those deals, the largest of which was the takeover of RJR/Nabisco by Kohlberg, Kravis, Roberts, a Wall Street buyout firm, for almost $23 billion. The number of deals increased each year until late 1987 when the market collapse forced them to slow. It was the M&A market that actually gave Wall Street its avaricious reputation during the 1980s because the fees the deal maker earned were so high. Wall Street deal makers became some of the most important names in business, ranking alongside corporate heads.

Continuing a trend begun in the 1970s, many of the takeovers were far from friendly. The 1980s became the decade of the hostile takeover and defensive measures used by many companies to fend them off. New terms appeared in the finance lexicon, suggesting all sorts of intriguing things, among them "raiders," "poison pills" and "shark repellent."

Paul Volcker's tenure at the Fed ended in 1987. He was succeeded by Alan Greenspan, another well-respected name on the Street. Then in the fall of 1987 the unthinkable appeared to happen again. The Dow Jones Industrial Average lost over 20 percent of its value in one day, October 19. The market, in the midst of the largest boom in its history, apparently had crashed again. And the phenomenon seemed to be worldwide. Many other markets actually lost more in percentage terms than Wall Street did. The immediate effects bode poorly for the Street. In addition to investor losses, many new issues were hurt badly by the rout, costing their underwriters substantial sums. As a result, many member firms laid off workers and cut back on costs.

In the aftermath of the market fall, a presidential commission

OPPOSITE

Go to jail, literally. Six hundred investment bankers and high-tech executives had a meeting and a party on Alcatraz Island in San Francisco in 1986.

Alan Greenspan succeeded Paul Volcker as chairman of the Fed in 1987. Greenspan remained committed to keeping inflation under check and became extremely popular on the Street as a result.

Another Crash? The newspapers certainly thought so as the market plunged more than 20 percent on October 19, 1987. The headlines proved to be somewhat exaggerated, fortunately for the Street and investors.

R eading about
the market drop.

W ithin a few days
of the market's
20 percent fall, crowds
began to gather outside
the visitor's gallery at
the NYSE to gain a
bird's-eye view of what
was happening on the
exchange.

T he market's plunge created an enormous
backlog of orders that had to be sorted out.
Here, a clerk sorts through the mass of sell orders
in the back room of Shearson Lehman Brothers.

What goes up. Traders are exuberant as the market gains back 180 of its lost points in late October. It would have to wait several years before beginning its upward movement again.

During the 1980s, Congress passed the Gramm-Rudman bill designed to force the government to maintain a balanced budget, something of a pipe dream at the time because of the Reagan administration's policies. Most commentators thought the bill politically expedient and nothing more—a way of winning votes. The British magazine *The Economist* was a bit more sarcastic, likening the bill to" a girl who can't say no so she puts on a chastity belt and throws away the key."

That sort of moment. A 6-foot walking Maalox can gives out free samples after the market rout in October.

headed by Nicholas Brady, the Treasury secretary, made several recommendations for the market that were adopted. The most noteworthy was the introduction of circuit breakers, levels that, once reached, would mandate an automatic closing of the NYSE until the problems could be sorted out. The breakers were introduced but ironically were not utilized much in the next ten years as the bull market resumed its upward spiral. But the enormous problems caused by the backlog of orders in 1929 and again in the late 1960s were not forgotten. Many traders and brokers realized that downward markets were seriously exacerbated by the inability of back rooms to keep up with the paperwork.

The junk bond market began to unravel in the late 1980s as the savings and loan crisis plunged the thrift institutions into serious difficulties—difficulties from which many would never recover. About $125 billion was eventually needed to set the industry aright. One of the problems was that many of the thrifts had bought junk bonds as investments, being allowed to do so under deregulation legislation introduced

Employees at the Philadelphia Stock Exchange have their IDs checked at a time of heightened security. After an angry client murdered a Miami stockbroker, security was increased at brokerages and exchanges around the country.

by the Reagan administration seven years before. Naturally, junk bonds were integrally tied to Milken and Drexel Burnham, and a clear tie became established between Wall Street and the small saver. It seemed that the Street was again benefiting from dubious practices that ultimately cost small investors their savings.

Boesky was eventually fined and served a prison term. Proceedings were begun against Milken as well. The decade of greed appeared to be at an end—but not before it was glorified one last time in *Wall Street*, the movie starring Michael Douglas. The shenanigans of corporate raiders and brokers trading on inside information was questionable, but it certainly did make for good entertainment.

OVERLEAF

Not again! Protestors outside the NYSE claiming that the financial system was near ruin at the end of the "decade of greed."

THE 1990s

AFTER THE SIGNIFICANT MARKET RISE
and the scandals of the 1980s, Wall Street needed
a breather. During the recession of 1990–1991,
the Dow managed to maintain the levels it had
achieved after recovering from the 1987 calamity
but still remained under 3,000. Even the wildest opti-
mists would not have thought that the averages would quadruple
within the next nine years.

The twentieth century had already witnessed some of history's
momentous changes, and the 1990s would certainly add to them. The
breakup of the Soviet Union in 1991 caused some concern among defense-related industries that traditionally relied on the Defense Department since the 1950s. But the economy emerged from the recession,
which proved to be relatively mild, and began to resume its strong performance. The first half of the decade was dominated by deregulatory
legislation that would help set the tone for the economy as the twenty-
first century approached. The easing of regulatory strictures on the utilities, banks, and railroads provided even more fuel for the merger and
acquisition fires that reemerged right after the recession ended.

Wall Street was setting its own house in order during the earlier
part of the decade. Michael Milken agreed to terms with the Justice Department and would be fined and sent to jail. Drexel Burnham itself

OPPOSITE

Diners celebrate the 200th anniversary of the NYSE on the floor itself. It was 200 years since the signing of the Buttonwood Agreement.

would close its doors after almost a century as a result of the junk bond scandal. Another scandal in the Treasury bond market would cost several senior Wall Street executives their jobs as the Fed detected collusion at Treasury bond auctions. But the ever-increasing market and the merger and acquisition boom kept the Street working overtime in order to meet demand.

The boom in the market and the strong economy began to whittle away at the budget deficit throughout the middle 1990s. When Bill Clinton took office in 1993, the budget deficit exceeded $300 billion and the U.S. national debt exceeded $4 trillion. However, the increased tax revenues generated by the strong economy helped the deficit fall almost every year thereafter. By the end of the decade, the deficit had turned into a surplus, the first in over four decades.

Former President Ronald Reagan, who in 1985 became the first sitting president to ever visit the NYSE, and former Soviet leader Mikhail Gorbachev in the gallery of the NYSE in 1992.

The mighty have fallen. Michael Milken makes his way through a crowd outside a New York courthouse after he has just agreed to pay a fine of $400 million. He eventually served three years in prison.

Ivan Boesky leaving a half-way house in Brooklyn at the end of his prison sentence.

Richard Breeden, chairman of the SEC, comments to reporters after Michael Milken was sentenced to prison.

A sign of things to come? After the Gulf War began, security was heightened on Wall Street. Here, an ID is checked outside an entrance to the NYSE.

OPPOSITE
Always time for a party. Wall Street welcomes Joint Chiefs of staff Chairman Colin Powell and Desert Storm Commander Norman Schwarzkopf in a ticker tape parade after the war was over.

*I*n another parade,
Wall Street welcomes
Nelson Mandela of
South Africa after
apartheid was dismantled.

In 1987, RJR/Nabisco became the largest takeover in history. In 1990, RJR Holdings issued bonds to help restructure the company.

74960KAA6 R   045744 POLLY.G...00023 A136845

REGISTERED

NUMBER

R 45744

Sections 1271 through 1275 of the Internal Revenue Code (and certain proposed Treasury regulations thereunder) require that this Security and any Secondary Securities issued in lieu of cash interest payments be treated as a single installment obligation which has been issued with original issue discount ("OID"). The issue date of such obligation is April 28, 1989. Because such obligation provides for the payment of interest at a variable rate, the yield to maturity of such obligation is a variable yield, and the amount of OID on such obligation is not presently determinable. Such amount of OID may be reallocated upon issuance of Secondary Securities in lieu of cash interest payments. The amount of OID allocable to the short accrual period is $0.1699 per $100 of principal amount, determined under proposed Treasury regulation Section 1.1275-5, using the exact method.

© S·C·B·Co.

RJR H

SENIOR

RJR Holdings Corp., a Delaw
the Indenture hereinafter referred to, for valu

POLLY & CO
PO BOX 1066
WALL STREET
NEW YORK NY

or registered assigns,
the principal sum of

on May 1, 2009.

Interest Payment Dates: The fourth anniversary of the first of the following to
or, in the event of the earlier occurrence of an Accelerated Conversion Date, the first s
Record Dates: The fifteenth Business Day immediately preceding each intere
Upon conversion of this Security into shares of common stock, $.01 par value
(as defined below) representing accrued and unpaid interest, and the Conversion Price (a
converted will be deemed to satisfy the Company's obligation to pay the principal amo
Reference is hereby made to the further provisions of this Security set forth or
of any series issued pursuant to the Indenture (referred to on the reverse hereof) are he

In Witness Whereof, the Company has ca
and a facsimile of its corporate seal to be affixe

Date:

TRUSTEE'S CERTIFICATE OF AUTHENTICATION

This is one of the Securities of the series designated herein issued under the Indenture described herein
THE CITIZENS AND SOUTHERN NATIONAL BANK,
as Trustee
or
BANKERS TRUST COMPANY,
as Authenticating Agent

By

Authorized Signature

© SECURITY-COLUMBIAN   UNITED STATES BANKNOTE COMPANY

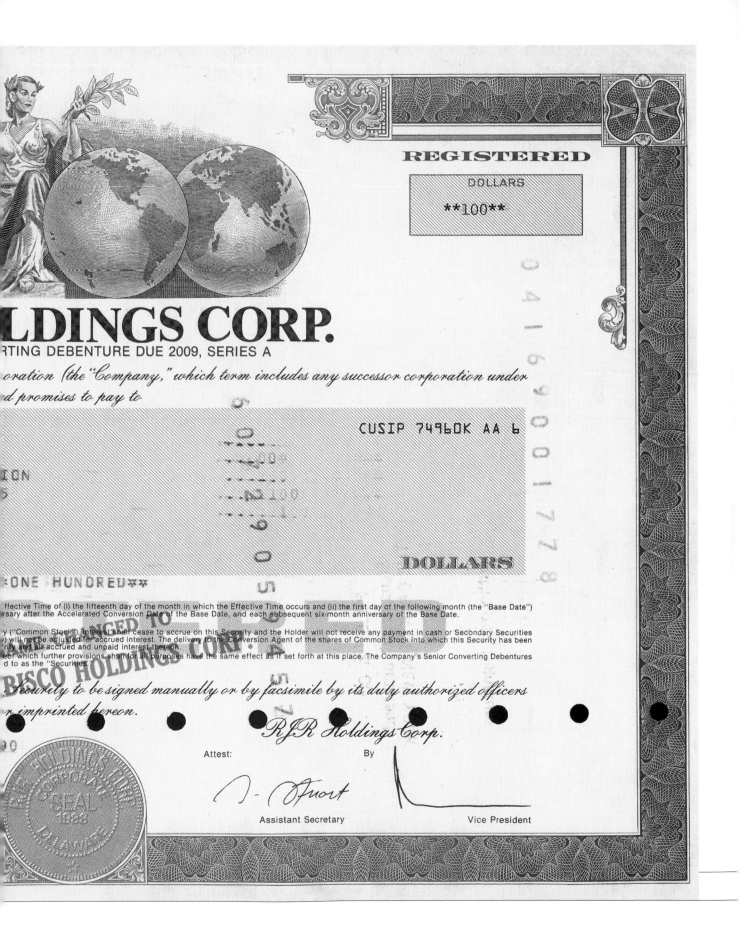

Wall Street suffered another one of its periodic terrorist shocks in the winter of 1993 when a huge bomb was set off in the World Trade Center in lower Manhattan. In the aftermath, security measures were tightened around the Street as well as the city in general.

The 1990s will be remembered for the extraordinary rise in the stock markets and the merger and acquisition mania that accompanied it. Both were continuations of the trend that began in the 1980s, interrupted by the market collapse in 1987. But they were not the only signs of a strong economy, only the most visible ones. The American economy proved to be the world's most resilient throughout the decade. The decade of greed gave way to the decade of boom. And ostentation was never far from view. Many of the consumer and financial magazines regularly reported on the price of the average yacht sale paid by Wall Street executives and the price of a bottle of wine at favorite Wall Street watering holes. The rising market created many 401K millionaires, those whose self-directed pension plans appreciated at double-digit rates of growth.

Because of the growth of mutual funds in the 1980s and 1990s, the "buy side" became as important on Wall Street as the "sell side." Peter Lynch helped build Fidelity's Magellen Fund into the world's largest mutual fund.

DOW JONES INDUSTRIAL AVERAGE, *1990-99*

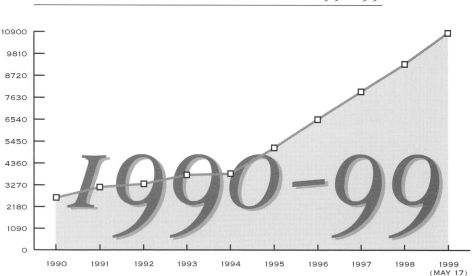

In 1993, a bomb explosion rocked the World Trade Center. After walking down the stairs of the building, survivors are led away by emergency workers. The bomb was set off in the parking garage below.

No pun intended? When a Dutch company listed its stock on the NYSE, it celebrated with festivities outside. Or was it a harbinger of things to come? The first major financial scandal was the tulip speculation in Holland in the seventeenth century.

The surging stock market spilled over into plain old-fashioned conspicuous consumption by the mid-1990s. Several steak houses frequented by the denizens of Wall Street reported brisk sales of bottles of French wine of up to $2,000 per bottle. In 1957, that was the price of a new car, fully loaded!

In the aftermath of a trading scandal, the venerable old house of Kidder Peabody finally closed its doors after being absorbed by Paine Webber. Kidder traced its origins back to Boston before the Civil War.

The phenomenal growth was unparalleled. It exceeded anything seen in the 1920s or the 1950s and 1960s and characterized a decade of wealth creation.

But the decade was not without its bumps along the way. Some of them proved to be quite substantial. The market suffered several temporary setbacks, each of which appeared to mark the end of the long rally. Some of the Dow's greatest one-day setbacks occurred during the late 1990s. Of the top ten days with the greatest net loss, nine occurred in 1997, 1998, and 1999. This is somewhat misleading because the days with the greatest *percentage* loss were still in the 1920s and 1930s. But it still shows that the market was extremely volatile during the last years of the century.

The most volatile days of the decade occurred in 1997 and 1998. On October 27, 1997, the market lost slightly over 7 percent of its value; and on August 31, 1998, it lost over 6 percent. International events played a prominent part in both drops. Serious economic conditions led to deteriorating currency and stock markets in both the Pacific Rim and Russia, and in both cases the market reacted strongly, fearing a worldwide recession or even depression. When it became clear that was not the case and that many developing economies looked to the United States as their locomotive of growth, the markets resumed their upward climb to

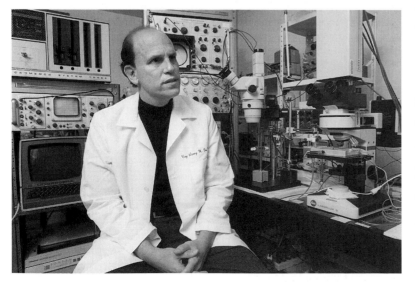

new records. But the lessons about volatility would not be forgotten.

Inflation was subdued in the 1990s, erasing the nightmarish memories of the early 1980s. Bond yields fell to their lowest levels since the mid-1960s and remained in a low range until the end of the decade. Yields became so low that many investors turned instead to the stock market. That led to even more stock buying than was expected.

*N*either wind nor
rain nor sleet.
*The NYSE remained open
during a major blizzard in
1996 but pedestrians and
traders were few.*

Morgan Stanley, which merged with Dean Witter in 1997, was one of the few major securities houses with offices away from the Wall Street area. This is its headquarters, located in Times Square.

The strong market led to a fundamental realignment of asset values across the spectrum. High-tech stocks dominated trading, and many of their prices defied gravity as well as logic. Traditional ways of valuing stocks were becoming difficult if not impossible since many of the new companies in the software and Internet businesses traded at very high prices based upon future expectations rather than current earnings. Expectations were based upon the idea that the world had entered a new economic age, dominated by information technology and the Internet.

The strong merger trend that began in the mid-1980s continued unabated in the 1990s, especially after 1992. Previous records were quickly broken as companies sought to merge. A great number of mergers between two companies in the same industry were announced, more than at any time since the 1920s. Notable mergers between Chase Manhattan and Chemical Bank, Citicorp and Travelers, and Daimler Benz and Chrysler, among many others, created companies with huge capitalizations. Wall Street rejoiced since the deals provided enormous fees for the deal makers. Speculators bought the stocks hoping for a huge merger payoff, adding more fuel to the market's rise.

Mergers on the Street itself also increased dramatically during the 1990s. Banks were allowed to acquire investment banks after more than sixty years of separation, and several bought brokers. The average Wall Street firm was becoming larger as the decade wore on, by either acquiring other brokers or being absorbed by a larger financial services company. Finally, in 1999 Goldman Sachs went public, selling shares for the first time. The last of Wall Street's major partnerships became accountable to shareholders.

New trading techniques appeared along with the Internet. Previously, only professional traders were known as day traders. But with the opening of new brokerage services on the net, many small investors could access their discount brokers with the click of a mouse and trade stocks for only a fraction of the commission charged by full-service brokers. This ushered in a whole new generation of day traders known as "e-traders." By moving in and out of stocks quickly, they added to the volume traded on the exchanges and often added volatility to the price of their favorite stocks. Contributing to their popularity was a whole generation of popular books showing how day trading could be profitable within a very short period of time.

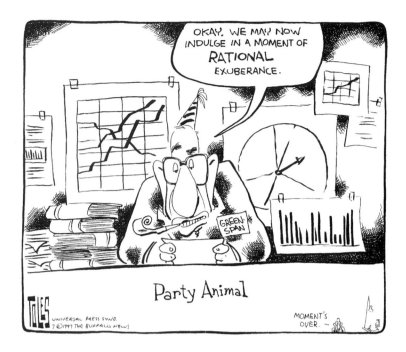

Party Animal

*I*n 1997, Fed Chairman Alan Greenspan rocked the markets when he claimed that investors were indulging in a bit of "irrational exuberance." But as the indices continued to climb, cartoonists began to have some fun with the phrase at his expense.

The markets took a tumble in October 1997, and Treasury Secretary Robert Rubin sought to calm the markets. Rubin said that despite the turmoil, the mechanisms established to deal with a market plunge were working well.

Legendary investor Warren Buffett and his Berkshire Hathaway Company became a bellwether of the stock market in the 1990s, with investors watching his market moves carefully.

Maria Bartiromo and Tyler Mathisen of CNBC. Financial news proliferated in the 1990s with national news stations such as CNBC, CNN, and the Bloomberg Network all providing constant information for investors.

As Microsoft's stock continued to rise in the 1990s, so too did the fortune of its chairman, Bill Gates. By the end of the decade, his holdings were worth somewhere between $70 billion and $80 billion. That amount would put him on equal footing with John D. Rockefeller, in adjusted terms.

OVERLEAF

More technological developments. In 1997, the NASDAQ announced the opening of its on-line service that provides information to executives of companies listed on the market about the trading of their stocks and those of their competitors.

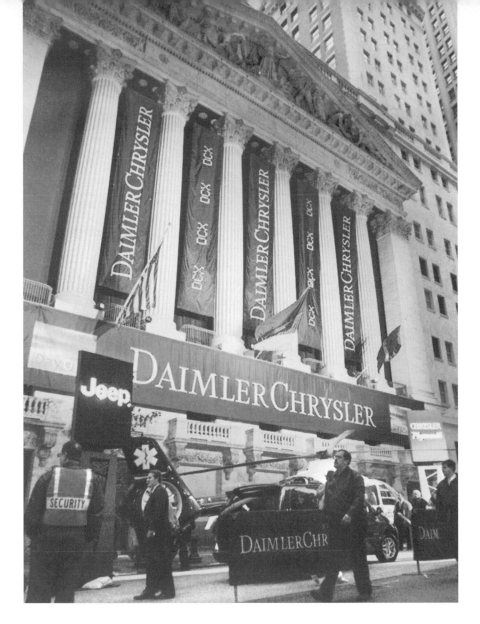

The NYSE celebrated the merger of Chrysler and Diamler by festooning the building with banners, illustrating the international importance of the new car manufacturer.

OPPOSITE

An options trader on the Chicago Board Options Exchange tries to make some sense out of the prices on Chrysler options after the company announced it was merged with by Daimler Benz. More mergers occurred in the 1990s than at any other time in history. And their value was greater than ever.

Financial news also proliferated during the 1990s. New radio and television networks were created to deal exclusively with financial events. Viewers and listeners were able to receive investment information around the clock, not just during NYSE trading hours. The constant flow of information helped to bring new investors to the market and helped chip away at some of Wall Street's mystique. As some of the invisible barriers surrounding companies and the markets fell, small investors flocked to the market. The market rally became much more broad based than any preceding it.

Derivatives suffered when the stock market suffered. On August 27, 1998, the Dow suffered its third biggest one-day trading loss in history. Here, futures traders at the Chicago Board of Trade look perplexed over the NYSE's loss.

OPPOSITE

No bull but not a bear either. A passerby rubs at the statue of the bull near the NYSE after a rough trading day in August 1998.

The precipitous market drop in August 1998 also brought down one of the Street's better known hedge funds, Long-Term Capital Management. Led by a veteran of the Treasury bond trading scandal of the early 1990s, the firm became overextended in its highly leveraged holdings and was near collapse when it was rescued by a group of banks and the Federal Reserve. Its problems came as something of a shock because it was assumed to use the most sophisticated risk management tools available.

The Clinton administration began to exercise some muscle in the mergers market by challenging some of the pending deals. The most noteworthy antitrust case in years was brought against the Microsoft Corporation, alleging that it was a monopoly and bullied the competition by not

Sanford Weill of the Travelers Corp. smiles after announcing that his company was merging with Citicorp. The new company also included Salomon Brothers which had previously merged with Smith Barney. The merger was made possible by a gradual relaxing of financial regulations during the late 1980s and early 1990s.

In a roaring bull market, events at securities houses became newsworthy. After the market plunged in the summer of 1998, Merrill Lynch announced that it would slash about 5 percent of its workforce. News crews rapidly descended upon its headquarters for comment.

A merger between the NASDAQ and the Amex was announced in 1998, combining the two different types of market into one enormous market-place to vie for business with the NYSE.

OVERLEAF

R obert Rubin, secre-tary of the Treasury under Clinton, was one of the most respected policy-makers in Washington besides Alan Greenspan. When he finally resigned in 1999, the markets suffered a momentary setback.

allowing its Windows users access to other Internet browsers. Microsoft fought the case in court. By the end of the century, its chairman, Bill Gates, was the richest man in the world because of the escalating value of the company's stock. The government also challenged Intel's monopoly in computer chips.

In the span of the century, Wall Street has seen many trends come and go. The century opened with the creation of U.S. Steel and ended with a fascination with stocks related to the Internet, a word not even in the dictionary in 1985. Within the course of its last 100 years, Wall Street has been through the industrial revolution, the post-industrial age, the computer revolution, and finally the information revolution based upon the Internet. It has seen war, terrorist attacks, inflation, scandals, and bear markets. Despite the many pitfalls, it played a central role in creating the American century, helping companies, governments, and investors participate in the greatest economic boom ever recorded.

Another record. The Dow hit 10,000 in March 1999, and a trader on the NYSE puts up ten fingers to celebrate.

OVERLEAF

On May 13, 1999 the Dow closed over 11,000. The index rose 225 on the day.

NYSE

THE NEW YORK STOCK EXCHANGE

The world puts its stock in u

```
46RH #MEXICO SELLS 343-0F
944R  U.S. TREASURY BALANC
592DH DJ NEWS HIGHLIGHTS:
945RH #MEXICO SELLS 161-0
NDU +215.92  VOLU 785.523
NDP 11004.96  UVOL 599
```

4:00:35

CETES AT 22.40 PCT VS

S AT FED FELL ON APRIL

JIA SETS CLOSING RECORD

CETES AT 21.60 PCT VS

00   TCK +322

I n 1999, Goldman Sachs, the last of the major Wall Street partnerships, went to market in a public offering. The issue ended the firm's 129 year history as a partnership. The company's headquarters is at 85 Broad Street.

One hundred years after the Dow was devised, only one stock that was included in the original average remained, General Electric. Originally purchased from Thomas Edison by J. P. Morgan, GE was an electrical supplier in its early years. One hundred years later, Edison would have had a difficult time recognizing his company, which had diversified into manufacturing and financial services among other endeavors. By the late 1990s, it had become the most highly capitalized company in the world.

Arthur Levitt, chairman of the SEC, faced many challenges in the 1990s, from scandals to new electronic marketplaces.

The old and the new. The popularity of trading via Internet encouraged many on-line brokers to go public. Here a representative of M.J. Meehan & Co. directs the trading in the new shares of DLJ Direct, the offspring of Donaldson, Lufkin & Jenrette.

Vice President Al Gore opening his presidential campaign with a
speech at the corner of Broad and Wall in 1999.

OVERLEAF

Brokers compare prices on the ticker tape in 1900, while contemporary brokers do the same
electronically in 1997.

DOW JONES INDUSTRIAL AVERAGE, *1900–99*

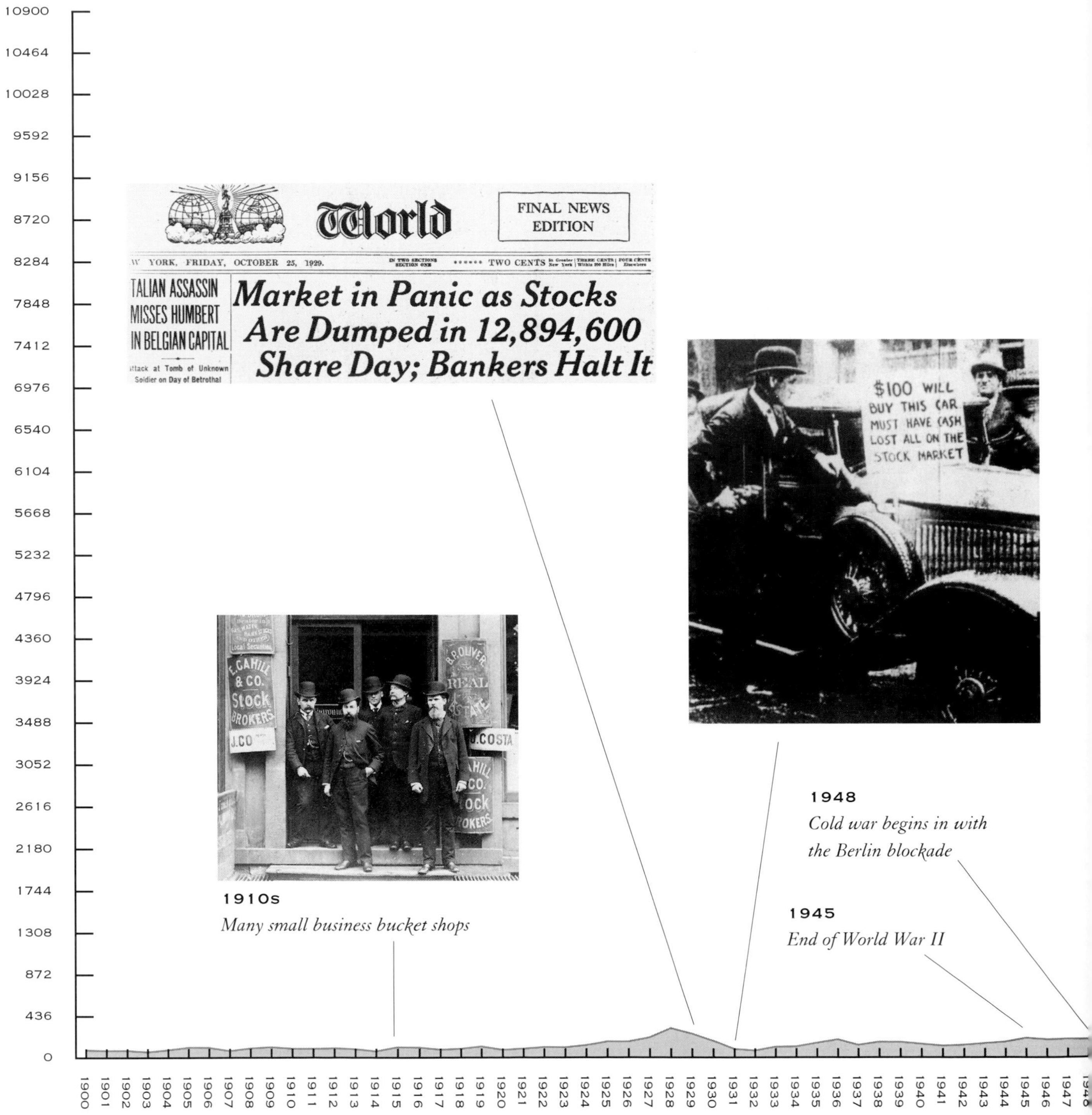

World
FINAL NEWS EDITION
W YORK, FRIDAY, OCTOBER 25, 1929.
TWO CENTS
TALIAN ASSASSIN MISSES HUMBERT IN BELGIAN CAPITAL
Attack at Tomb of Unknown Soldier on Day of Betrothal
Market in Panic as Stocks Are Dumped in 12,894,600 Share Day; Bankers Halt It
$100 WILL BUY THIS CAR MUST HAVE CASH LOST ALL ON THE STOCK MARKET
E. CAHILL & CO. Stock BROKERS
B.P. OLIVER REAL ESTATE
J.CO
J.COSTA
1910s
Many small business bucket shops
1945
End of World War II
1948
Cold war begins in with the Berlin blockade
10900
10464
10028
9592
9156
8720
8284
7848
7412
6976
6540
6104
5668
5232
4796
4360
3924
3488
3052
2616
2180
1744
1308
872
436
0
1900 1901 1902 1903 1904 1905 1906 1907 1908 1909 1910 1911 1912 1913 1914 1915 1916 1917 1918 1919 1920 1921 1922 1923 1924 1925 1926 1927 1928 1929 1930 1931 1932 1933 1934 1935 1936 1937 1938 1939 1940 1941 1942 1943 1944 1945 1946 1947 1948

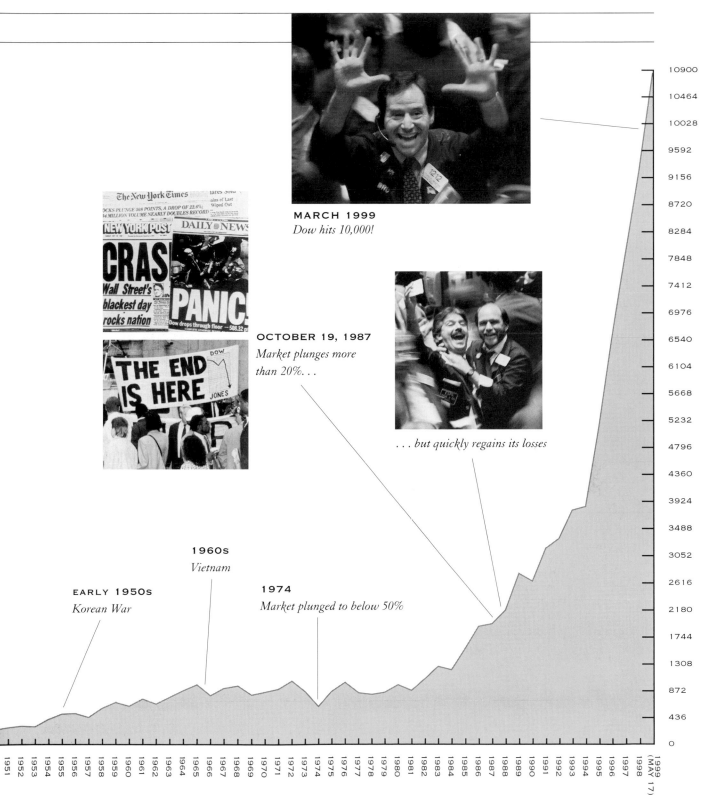

MARCH 1999
Dow hits 10,000!

OCTOBER 19, 1987
*Market plunges more
than 20%. . .*

. . . but quickly regains its losses

1960s
Vietnam

EARLY 1950s
Korean War

1974
Market plunged to below 50%

10900
10464
10028
9592
9156
8720
8284
7848
7412
6976
6540
6104
5668
5232
4796
4360
3924
3488
3052
2616
2180
1744
1308
872
436
0

1951 1952 1953 1954 1955 1956 1957 1958 1959 1960 1961 1962 1963 1964 1965 1966 1967 1968 1969 1970 1971 1972 1973 1974 1975 1976 1977 1978 1979 1980 1981 1982 1983 1984 1985 1986 1987 1988 1989 1990 1991 1992 1993 1994 1995 1996 1997 1998 1999 (MAY 17)

INDEX

F

Federal Reserve, 4, 29, 81, 110, 119, 130, 156
First Boston Corp., 50
Fisher, Irving, 34
Fraunces Tavern, 101

G

Gates, Bill, 149, 159
Geneen, Harold, 88
General Electric, 163
General Motors, 23, 80
German terrorism, 11
Glass, Carter, 45
Glass-Steagall Act, 45, 50
Go-go years, 87
Goldman Sachs, 147, 162
Gorbachev, Mikhail, 130
Gore, Al, 165
Gould, Jay, 5
Graf Zeppelin, 26–27
Gramm-Rudman Act, 122
Grand Central Station, 109
Grasso, Richard, 146
Great Depression, 29, 39–42, 47
Greenspan, Alan, 119, 125, 147
Gulf & Western Industries, 92

H

Haack, Robert, 90
Henry Clews & Co., 36
High-tech companies, 113

Hoodlum Saint (film), 68
Hoover, Herbert, 40, 48
Hutton & Co., 69
Hutton, W. D., 69

I

Income tax, 5
Inflation:
 in 1940s, 66
 in late 1960s and early 1970s, 97, 100
Influenza epidemic, 6
Insider trading, 113, 116
Intel, 113
International Harvester, 1
Investment pools, 23, 46
Iran hostage crisis, 100
ITT, 88

J

J. P. Morgan & Co., 28
Japan, 110
Jazz Age, 17, 39
Junk bond market, 112, 119, 124–125
Junk bond scandal, 130

K

Kann, Peter, 146
Kennedy, John F., 87
Kennedy, Joseph P., 29, 49

in 1960s, 91

and brokers, 12

and Chrysler-Daimler
    merger, 153

and Crash of 1929, 29, 30

and Crash of 1987, 121

and curb market, 20

in Great Depression, 47, 49,
    51–53

and insider trading scandal, 113

and panic of 1907, 3

Ronald Reagan at, 130

and reforms, 57–58, 124

and short selling, 40–42

200th anniversary of, 128–129

women in, 61

during World War II, 62–63

New York Times, 5

Noble, Henry, 6

Northern Securities Company, 1

NYSE (*see* New York Stock
    Exchange)

O

OPEC, 97

Over-the-counter market, 20

P

Paine Webber, 141

Panic(s):
    of 1903, 2
    of 1907, 2

Pecora, Ferdinand, 44, 45

Pecora hearings, 41–46

Penn Central Railroad, 100

Ponzi, Charles, 18

Powell, Colin, 132

Predator's Ball, 112

Prohibition, 48

Prohibition Amendment, 6

Pujo hearings, 3–5

R

Rapid American Corporation, 88

Raskob, John, 23, 46, 47

RCA, 26, 80

Reagan, Ronald, 130

Reagan administration, 110, 125

Regan, Don, 112

Richard Whitney & Co., 57

Riklis, Menshulem, 88

RJR/Nabisco, 119, 136

Rockefeller, John D., 2, 3, 149

Roosevelt, Franklin D., 41, 48,
    49, 59

Roosevelt, Teddy, 1, 3

Roosevelt administration, 64

Rubin, Robert, 148

S

Salomon Brothers, 156

Savings and loan crisis, 124

Schwarkopf, Norman, 132

SEC (*see* Securities and Exchange
    Commission)

Securities Act of 1933, 48, 49

PHOTO CREDITS

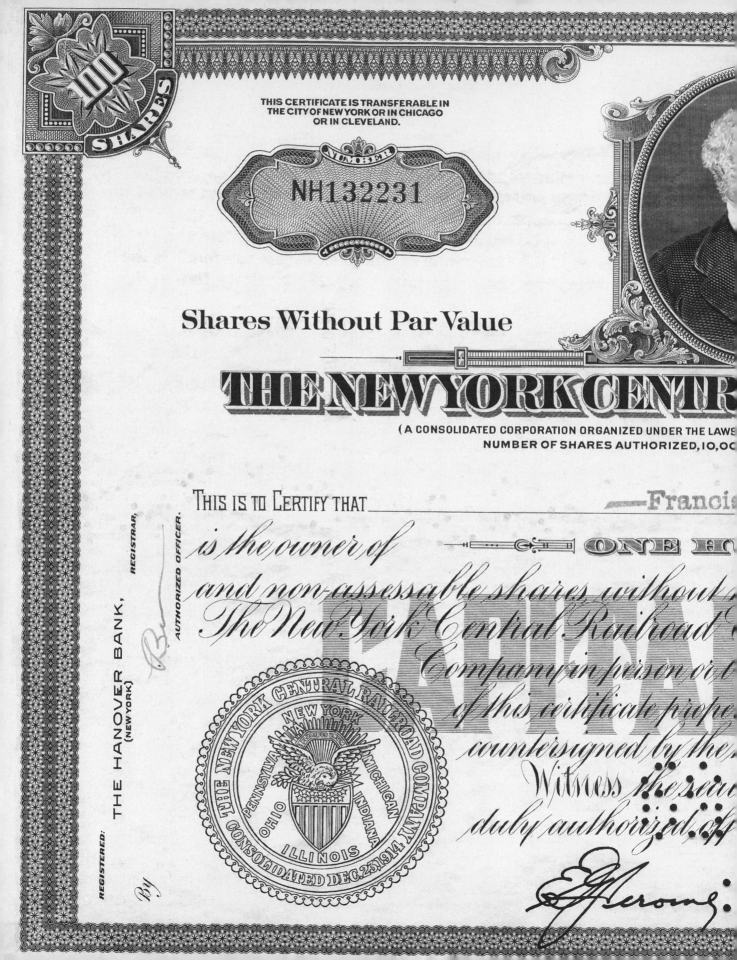

100 SHARES

NUMBER

NH132231

Shares Without Par Value

THE NEW YORK CENTR

(A CONSOLIDATED CORPORATION ORGANIZED UNDER THE LAWS
NUMBER OF SHARES AUTHORIZED, 10,00

THIS IS TO CERTIFY THAT ———————————— —Francis

is the owner of ONE HU

and non-assessable shares without

The New York Central Railroad

Company in person or

of this certificate prope

countersigned by the

Witness the

duly authorized off

REGISTERED:

THE HANOVER BANK,
(NEW YORK)

REGISTRAR,

AUTHORIZED OFFICER.

By

THE NEW YORK CENTRAL RAILROAD COMPANY
NEW YORK
PENNSYLVANIA · MICHIGAN · OHIO · INDIANA · ILLINOIS
CONSOLIDATED DEC. 23, 1914